# The Art of Computer Modeling for Business Analytics

# The Art of Computer Modeling for Business Analytics

## Paradigms and Case Studies

Gerald Feigin, PhD

**BEP** BUSINESS EXPERT PRESS

*The Art of Computer Modeling for Business Analytics: Paradigms and Case Studies*

Copyright © Business Expert Press, LLC, 2016

First published in 2016 by
Business Expert Press, LLC
222 East 46th Street, New York, NY 10017
www.businessexpertpress.com

ISBN-13: 978-1-63157-375-0 (paperback)
ISBN-13: 978-1-63157-376-7 (e-book)

Business Expert Press Quantitative Approaches to Decision Making
Collection

Collection ISSN: 2163-9515 (print)
Collection ISSN: 2163-9582 (electronic)

Cover and interior design by S4Carlisle Publishing Services
Private Ltd., Chennai, India

First edition: 2016

10 9 8 7 6 5 4 3 2 1

Printed in the United States of America.

# Dedication

*For Juliette, Jennifer, and Amanda*

# Abstract

In just about every sphere of business today, companies routinely utilize computer models to help make decisions. These models take many forms, from simple spreadsheets to sophisticated computer simulations. They may be bespoke models built for a specific company or they may be commercial software packages designed to be used by many different companies. They can be intended for one-time use to help decision makers think through a significant business decision or they can be tools designed for ongoing use within a company. They may be static or dynamic, deterministic or stochastic.

The specific reasons for building a model are as varied as the models themselves, but the chief underlying reason is to assess the impact of a decision or a set of decisions on business performance. Based on that assessment, model users will make recommendations and take actions. The tacit assumption is that the model captures the relevant factors at a sufficient level of detail to make accurate projections and that, therefore, the conclusions drawn from the model are reasonable. The validity of the model thus depends on a host of judgments that the model builder makes in constructing the model—some transparent, others implicit. These judgments are what make building a computer model more of an art than a science.

This book is about constructing and using computer models to help decision makers in the business world make more informed decisions. It is intended to provide useful paradigms and case studies for individuals who are interested in building effective decision models—ones that will get used to drive important business decisions. The focus is on practice, not theory. In particular, the book does not focus on the underlying methods for building models—for example, how to construct a discrete event simulation, how to solve a linear program, or how to perform a multivariable linear regression.

My goal rather is to demonstrate, mainly through case studies, how to build effective models quickly and inexpensively, using software that is widely available and often free. It is meant as a practical guide, informed by my experience building such models for an array of businesses in diverse industries.

# Keywords

business analytics, computer modeling, customer analytics, data analytics, decision modelling, decision models, mathematical modeling, operational modeling, optimization, simulation, supply chain management, supply chain modeling.

# Contents

# Preface

In just about every sphere of business today, companies routinely utilize computer models to help make decisions. These models take many forms, from simple spreadsheets to sophisticated computer simulations. They may be bespoke models built for a specific company or they may be commercial software packages designed to be used by many different companies. They can be intended for one-time use to help decision makers think through a significant business decision or they can be tools designed for ongoing use within a company. They may be static or dynamic, deterministic or stochastic.

The specific reasons for building a model are as varied as the models themselves, but the chief underlying reason is to assess the impact of a decision or a set of decisions on business performance. Based on that assessment, model users will make recommendations and take actions. The tacit assumption is that the model captures the relevant factors at a sufficient level of detail to make accurate projections and that, therefore, the conclusions drawn from the model are reasonable. The validity of the model thus depends on a host of judgments that the model builder makes in constructing the model—some transparent, others implicit. These judgments are what make building a computer model more of an art than a science.

This book is about constructing and using computer models to help decision makers in the business world make more informed decisions. It is intended to provide useful paradigms and case studies for individuals who are interested in building effective decision models—ones that will get used to drive important business decisions. The focus is on practice, not theory. In particular, the book does not focus on the underlying methods for building models—for example, how to construct a discrete event simulation, how to solve a linear program, or how to perform a multivariable linear regression. There are many books on these topics and there is little need to add to this already substantial literature.

My goal rather is to demonstrate, mainly through case studies, how to build effective models quickly and inexpensively, using software that is widely available and often free. It is intended as a practical guide, informed by my experience building such models for an array of businesses in diverse industries. My focus is on building models that will be used, not those that will be admired as theoretically interesting. Operations research, and the modeling that is central to its purpose, must be grounded in finding practical, workable solutions, not theory. Jagjit Singh, an early operations researcher, wrote:

> A worker in the field of operations research, unlike the fundamental researcher, cannot wait for posterity to prove him right. He cannot, like Leonardo da Vinci, Galois, or Babbage, spell out his ideas, as it were, over the heads of his contemporaries, hoping that they would be hailed a century or two later. He is pragmatic and is interested in having his way and his ideas implemented here and now. If he does not, he labors in vain. . .Operations research that is not acted upon at once is like an unborn idea that is never missed.[1]

Unfortunately, just as the graveyard is full of indispensable people, our old files are filled with impressive models that never quite saw the light of day. I hope that this book, through examples of both successes and failures, can help steer model builders away from the rocky shoals that doom most models.

The title of this book is an homage to Donald Knuth's classic multi-volume text "*The Art of Computer Programming.*"[2] Knuth explained what he intended by the use of the word "art" in the title by saying:

> When I speak about computer programming as an art, I am thinking primarily of it as an art form, in an aesthetic sense. The chief goal of my work as educator and author is to help people learn how to write beautiful programs....My feeling is that when we prepare a program, it can be like composing poetry or music; as Andrei Ershov has said, programming can give us both intellectual and emotional satisfaction, because it is a real achievement to master complexity and to establish a system of consistent rules.[3]

In using the word "art" in the title of this book, I too mean it in the sense that Knuth meant it. But the challenges of creating a useful computer model go beyond the formulating of an algorithm and its implementation in code. Perhaps the biggest challenge in computer modeling is distilling the business problem we are interested in addressing in all of its richness and complexity down to its essence. The art here is in capturing just the right set of aspects of the problem at just the right level of detail, so that the model solution provides valuable insight without becoming unnecessarily complex or difficult to solve. Finding the right balance between fidelity and complexity is one of the keys to good computer modeling and it is an art rather than a science because there is no formula or algorithm for finding that balance. It requires judgment, experience, and above all, imagination. If there is one thing I want readers of this book to take from it is that computer modeling can be richly rewarding. It provides the aesthetic satisfaction that comes from constructing an elegant model and the added satisfaction that it has been utilized to make practical decisions. This last point is important because if the model is not utilized, the degree of satisfaction derived is greatly diminished.

The other term in the title that is worth commenting on is "business analytics." A cynic might say that I've included the term only to capitalize on its current popularity. That is not entirely false but the title without this qualification is too broad. Computer modeling as a generic term could be used to denote the use of computers for almost any purpose. And the emphasis in this book is on solving business problems—specifically problems related to operations and planning—through the use of computer models. If there is anything at all to the concept of business analytics, it must be that it is concerned with how to use the power of computers to analyze and solve business problems. If this definition is accurate, then I would argue that computer models are an integral part of business analytics. For one cannot utilize the power of computers to analyze business problems without having some sort of computer model. Unfortunately, in the cacophony that makes up much of business analytics marketing, the discussion of computer models is often lost. One objective of this book is to help bring computer modeling front and center to the discussion of business analytics, where it belongs.

This book is intended for students of business who have an interest in understanding how computer models are designed, built, and utilized to help make business decisions. I have deliberately excluded equations from this book in the hope of appealing to a wider audience than might typically venture into this terrain. The first chapter makes a number of general points about computer modeling that might be too abstract for readers unfamiliar with the subject. For such individuals, it might be better to start immediately with the case studies in Chapters 2 to 9 and then return to Chapter 1 afterwards.

## Endnotes

1. Singh (1968).
2. Knuth (1995).
3. Knuth (1974).

# Acknowledgments

I am grateful to the many friends and colleagues who graciously provided valuable comments on the initial draft of this book and who engaged in helpful discussions on various topics: Ken Brooks, Dan Connors, Alex de Sherbinin, Brenda Dietrich, J. P. Fasano, Nagesh Gavirneni, James Hansen, Kaan Katircioglu, Burak Kazaz, Tan Miller, Ashok Mukherjee, Jim Schor, and David Yao.

# CHAPTER 1

# Introduction

## 1.1 What Is a Computer Model?

A simple question that deserves a simple answer. My answer is that a computer model is three essential things: a mathematical model and solution approach, an implementation of this model in software, and the data necessary to instantiate the model so as to make it of practical value.

A computer model starts out as a mathematical idea, a way of framing a real-world problem in terms of mathematical objects that we can manipulate to obtain results. A queueing model is a good example. The dynamics of how queues are formed and evolve in any real-world situation are highly complex. Take, for example, a traffic jam on a highway or the queue at an airport check-in counter. But if we abstract the notion of customers arriving to a system as a stochastic process and similarly abstract the service of these customers as another stochastic process, we can begin to model the dynamics of queues using the language of probability theory. By doing so and by making assumptions about the arrival and service processes, we can obtain useful formulas that predict statistical properties of queues such as the average waiting time and the average number in queue. Or when formulas are not available, we can utilize computer simulation to evaluate the performance of these systems.

Another example is a linear programming model of a production system. Modern manufacturing facilities are highly complex and the effective operation of them requires balancing competing objectives—for example, the desire to keep lead times and work-in-process (WIP) low and the desire to make sure that bottleneck work centers are fully utilized. Suppose we wish to provide a plant manager with a tool that will help him decide the right mix of products to produce given a forecast for products and constraints on material and capacity. If we make a series of simplifying assumptions about the production process, we can formulate the decision problem that the plant manager is faced with as a linear programming problem where the objective is, for example, to maximize profit subject to the constraints on material and capacity. The simplifying assumptions require stating the objective and the constraints as linear functions of the decision variables. But once these assumptions are made, the resulting linear programming model can be solved using well-established algorithms, such as the simplex algorithm. The solution to the linear program can then be interpreted as production plan that the plant manager can understand and use.

The mathematical formulation of the problem is one of the key first steps in creating a computer model. But it is not the computer model itself. The mathematical model exists separately from its realization in software. In rare cases, a mathematical model by itself without being implemented in software may provide practical insight in business contexts. For example, the approximate formula for the average waiting time in a single server queue can provide useful managerial insight into operations without resorting to a computer program. But in the vast majority of cases today, the mathematical model only becomes useful when it is transformed into software. That process—of taking an abstract mathematical model and converting it into a useful software program—is the next major step in the construction of a computer model. The challenges of implementing the model in software are not in any way less significant than the mathematical modeling itself. There are a host of issues that the software developer needs to pay attention to, not least the efficiency of the code.

But the computer model is not just the software implementation of a mathematical model. The key final ingredient in a computer model is the data needed to populate it. Without accurate data, the model is just an abstraction. The collection of data is an integral component in bringing a computer model to life and making it truly useful. In this view, data collection is not an ancillary activity to be undertaken after the mathematical model has been formulated and the computer code has been written. It is a core part of the model and needs to be undertaken in concert with the other model-building activities.

## 1.2    The Process of Computer Modeling

The process of creating a computer model is highly iterative. The basic steps are illustrated in Figure 1.1. The first two steps—formulate and design—involve understanding the business problem that needs to be solved, formulating a mathematical model and solution approach, and designing the software solution. Build/test/collect data involves coding, debugging, verification, and data collection. The validation/analyze step focuses on using the model to analyze the business problem, first to validate the model and then to examine alternative scenarios. The final phase, synthesize, requires interpretation of the model results in the broad business context and layering on additional considerations that the model may not have explicitly addressed.

### Formulation and Design

The first step is to be clear on what business questions the model is intended to address. It is not too strong a statement to say that all modeling decisions rest on this understanding, so it is worth spending a good deal of time thinking this through before starting the model building process. It often becomes clear in this process that more than one model may be needed to address all of the questions. That is often a better choice than trying to expand the scope and/or detail of a model so that it can address all questions, and in so doing, creating a model that is too difficult and complex for people to understand and use.

Once the questions the model is intended to address have been articulated, two principal choices need to be made: the scope of the model and the level of detail captured in the model. By scope, I mean the choice of

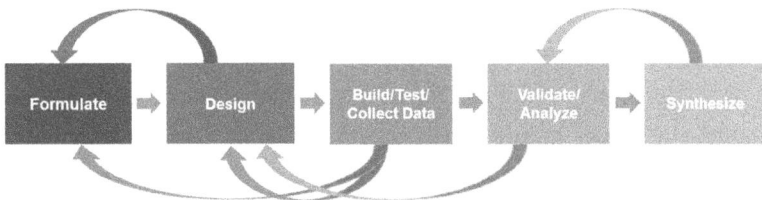

Figure 1.1 The steps in creating and utilizing a computer model. The process is highly iterative

the physical and logical components of the business which we are going to include within the model and those which we are going to exclude. By level of detail, I mean at what level of granularity the physical, logical, and temporal components of the business will be represented in the model. The physical components of the model are those objects that represent physical infrastructure, such as manufacturing locations, distribution centers, or retail outlets. The logical components of the model include operating constraints, decision rules, and behavioral logic. An example of an operating constraint is that a given product must be sourced from a given manufacturing site. An example of a decision rule is: When a piece of equipment in a factory becomes free, what product does it process next? An example of behavioral logic is: When a piece of equipment fails, how long does it fail for, what other equipment does it impact, and what happens when the equipment is repaired? The temporal components of the model include the time granularity represented in the model (e.g. days, weeks, months, or years), the time duration of the model, and the determination of which components of the model will vary with time and which will remain constant.

When describing the scope of a model, it is important to describe not only what will be included and excluded from the model, but the boundary conditions at the interface between what is modeled and what is not. In particular, it is necessary to make clear the events and triggers that occur at the boundaries that serve as sources and sinks for the model. For example, if one were constructing a model of port operations, there are two obvious boundaries to be considered: arrival of tractor trailers to the port to discharge, or load containers and ships that arrive at berths to be loaded or unloaded with containers. Performance of the port will depend significantly on the assumptions made about how ships and tractor trailers arrive.

In reaching a decision on model scope and level of detail, the modeler must grapple with two fundamental tradeoffs that exist in constructing a useful decision model. First, the more detail that is incorporated into a model, the greater its fidelity, but the more data that the model requires as input, the more complicated the physical and logical descriptions of the model become. Second, the greater the scope of the model, the more questions that it can be used to address and the larger the potential number of users, but the more complicated the model becomes to design. In general, the price of greater model accuracy and scope is greater time and cost to develop, use, and maintain. There is a point at which a model becomes so complex and difficult to understand that it loses its usefulness. There is also a point, usually reached much earlier, at which adding detail to a model results in diminishing returns in terms of increased model accuracy. Experienced modelers accept this almost as a truism but there is little beyond anecdote to demonstrate this phenomenon.

The other important point to emphasize is that model design should take data availability into account. Too often, I see models developed where the data required to drive the model is just an afterthought, as though data collection is subordinate to the model development process. In this view, the development of the model can occur before or in isolation to the data collection activities. It is precisely such thinking that leads to so many models never being put into use. Without considering the availability of data necessary to populate a model, a model developer risks developing a model which no one can use because the data necessary to run the model does not exist or requires too much effort or cost to collect. In all of the modeling work I have done, the effort to construct the model has never been the major bottleneck; collecting data almost always is.

The design, development, and testing of the model itself in software, and the collection, cleaning, analysis, and processing of input data needed to validate and run the model are separate but closely intertwined and must be performed in concert. Model development and data collection should ideally follow a process of triangulation, where the model developer is made aware at the outset of data that is easily accessible, data that is more difficult but possible to gather, and data that is going to be impossible to collect, given time and budget constraints. This information should be used in designing the model. The model developer may realize that certain data that is critical to the model may not exist and may be difficult or impossible to gather and these constraints should be addressed early on in the development process. Usually some creative thinking will lead to an approach to circumvent the constraints. At the same time as the model is being designed and developed, efforts should be underway to collect, clean, analyze, and process the data that will be used to populate the model. By examining this data closely, understanding what is readily available and what is not, the model developer can incorporate this knowledge in the design of the model.

Once these basic design choices are made, the modeler can then begin to think about some of the more tactical questions about model building: what the best technology to construct the model is, what specific software should be used, what the user interface should look like, what data will be necessary to input into the model, and what the principal model outputs should be. There are trade-offs in these decisions as well and answers will depend on a host of factors, not least the model builder's familiarity with different modeling techniques and software.

### Building the Model

A computer model is software and as such, its development should follow standard software development practices. My intention is not to rehash these practices, which the reader can find in many books devoted to this subject.[1] Having said that, I will add that computer models are often developed on a shoe-string budget with a small development group and on a short timeline, so rigorously following software development practices becomes difficult or impossible. Shortcuts are inevitable. For example, defining software requirements and the creation of extensive test cases are activities that are often abbreviated or skipped altogether.[2] I am not advocating that these steps be skipped, but just acknowledging that constraints often require us to impose shortcuts. The ideal model developer is one who is cognizant of best practices in software development but is not a stickler for following them and can judge which shortcuts are necessary or appropriate in a given situation.

### The Necessity and Impossibility of Model Verification and Validation

Verification and validation are two critical steps in the development of a computer model. Verification is the process of confirming that the model as implemented in software does what the model designer intends. Validation is the process of confirming that the model is a reasonable representation of the real-world system being modeled. Verification and validation are always necessary but also impossible to perform thoroughly for any complex system.

Model verification is nothing more or less than debugging a piece of software. This starts with the straightforward process of correcting syntactical errors and simple logical errors. But as anyone involved in software quality assurance knows, the process becomes much more challenging after this stage. The problem is that, as with any complex piece of software, the number of possible combinations of inputs to the computer model is enormous. Beyond the combinatorial challenge of enumerating and testing all corner cases, there is the more vexing problem of being able to say with certainty whether the model output, for any given set of inputs, is correct or not. Making sure that the model works correctly in all situations becomes virtually impossible in any finite period of time with a finite number of resources.

Even more troubling is that for a complex model, there may be no easy way of confirming whether the model results are correct or not. Many years ago, I worked for a short period as a product manager for a small software company. The software the company sold was designed to calculate optimal inventory targets for complex manufacturing and distribution networks. If you gave an input of a description of a supply chain to the software, it would calculate supposedly optimal inventory targets for each stocking location in the network. I say supposedly because the problem the software was solving was a non-linear stochastic optimization problem, the general solution to which, for arbitrary supply chains, does not exist. To be sure, there are special cases for which optimal solutions can be found but for general networks, there is no closed-form analytical solution. We developed heuristics to solve the problem and implemented these heuristics in software. But verification became a particularly thorny problem.

For a given test case, if the solution to the problem was not known, how could we verify that the software was outputting a correct solution? Performing the calculation by hand was not an option. Writing separate code to independently confirm the calculations is time-consuming and also leads to a potential infinite regress: If the results of the two pieces of code don't agree, then what? Write a 3rd piece of code? At the end of the day, the criteria we adopted for the many test cases in which the optimal solution was not known analytically, was this: Is the solution not obviously wrong? In other words, in examining the solution, could we find something that was obviously wrong with it? If not, the test case passed. (By the way, if the test case did not pass, we were still left with the question of figuring out whether it was the algorithm that was at fault or its implementation in software, another vexing challenge.)

These criteria were obviously wrong (who is to judge what is obviously wrong?) but in the absence of an alternative, this is what we were left with. Needless to say, this did not sit well with me. Consider a customer who uses the software on which he is basing multi-million dollar inventory investment decisions that will affect customer service levels and profitability. The software tells him the optimal way to allocate inventory in his supply chain. Our criterion for judging that the solution was optimal was that it is not obviously wrong. Caveat emptor.

In this situation, there was an approach that we could have used to independently verify that the solution the software calculated was at least partially correct. That was to construct a discrete event simulation of the supply chain using the recommended inventory targets as input and measuring the achieved service levels. This would not confirm that the solution was optimal but would at least give some confidence that the algorithms were working correctly. However, the CEO opted against investing in building such a simulation, so this approach went untried.

In most practical situations, we find ourselves developing a computer model rapidly and with extremely limited time and resources. Time is of the essence and there is little room for following the standard QA procedures of writing extensive test cases to verify model output. In these situations, verification, beyond the process of fixing syntax errors and basic checking that the model runs to completion, simply does not happen. Or rather, it happens only once the model starts being used and users start questioning the output. At that point, because adequate verification has not been done, the developers scramble to figure out if the problem is due to a logical error in the code. This results in one of three outcomes: (1) The model is correctly calculating the outputs given the inputs. The problem is that an input was incorrectly specified. (2) The model is correctly calculating the outputs given the inputs but the model design has a problem (or feature) that leads to the problematic output. (3) The model is incorrectly calculating the outputs and needs to be corrected.

The problem with insufficient verification is that it can erode confidence in the model. As more errors are identified by users, who become in effect an informal, imperfect, and highly vocal QA team, and if those errors turn out to be due to programming mistakes, people tend to question the model's integrity and interest in the model can fade quickly. It is therefore worth doing more than just a rudimentary job of verification, although the right amount is going to depend on how much time you have and how many resources are at your disposal.

Model validation is arguably much more difficult than verification. This is a process that is unique to computer modeling and is not applicable to software development in general. It has thus not received as much attention by computer scientists as software verification has. At a high level, model validation is the process of confirming that the model adequately represents the real-world system that it is modeling. A priori, we know that complete validation will fail—there will always be differences between the model's output and the observed results of the real system. The question is how much of a discrepancy there is between the model and the real system, and whether we can live with these discrepancies.

To perform a validation, typically we identify one or more "base cases". These are scenarios or model instances about which we know something in the real system. Often, a base case is a "business-as-usual" type of scenario because the data that we have about the real system corresponds to a past period of system evolution for which data has been collected. For example, if we have built a simulation model of a factory, to validate the simulation we may examine the cycle times, equipment utilizations, and factory throughput over the last year and compare these to the simulation results using inputs that correspond to the factory operation over this period. If the simulation predicts cycle times, equipment utilizations, and throughputs within, say 5%, of the real factory, we declare victory.

Validation is time-consuming and arduous, but at least making an effort to do it is absolutely necessary. What constitutes adequate validation will depend on a number of factors, not least the amount of time available and quantity of data available from the real system.

One of the inevitable challenges in validation is deciding whether the results of the model are close enough to the real system's performance. And if they are not close enough, there is the difficult process of figuring out how to change the model so that it closes the gap sufficiently. This often is not obvious and may require multiple iterations before any improvement is observed.

There is a temptation, when the model results do not match actual system performance, to tweak model parameters to obtain a better fit. At a minimum, this should be done in a transparent way and should be justifiable in a way which an executive sponsor will understand. Arbitrary fudge factors are never a good choice. One major problem is that you may end up with a model overly tuned to a base case that compares well with the real system. But when you start to use the model to explore other scenarios for which there is no comparison in the real system, the results may not make sense.

## 1.3    The Challenges of Model Acceptance

Even after a model has been constructed and validated, significant challenges remain in getting users and other interested parties to utilize the model and to act on its recommendations. Early in my career, I did some work for the IBM PC Company in Europe. I was working in the research division of IBM at the time and we had developed a model for the production planners to use. After we developed the model, I made a trip to IBM's PC manufacturing plant in Greenock, Scotland, to meet with the planners and explain its use. I remember little about the model or its purpose. But I do remember the reaction of the Scottish employees in the department I was visiting when they heard I was coming with a model. There was only one kind of model in their minds, and that was an attractive young person wearing fashionable clothes. And so, the running joke while I was visiting was that my model was a big disappointment. They wanted a fashion model, not a computer model. They thought this double entendre was hugely entertaining and I politely smiled each time someone felt the urge to make another lame joke in this vein.

After my visit, though, I realized that I would have been better off bringing a fashion model for all the lasting good that my computer model did. I naively believed that if I constructed a useful tool that would be helpful to the planners in doing some aspect of their jobs, they would embrace it. The model that I presented to them was received with graciousness and then promptly forgotten like a useless birthday gift. This was the first of many practical lessons about modeling that I have learned over the years. Building a better mouse trap will usually not cause people to beat a path to your door. Rather, if using the better mouse trap requires relinquishing a tried and tested, if not very effective, mouse trap, people will resist at all costs the adoption of the new one. Jay Forrester, a pioneer of system dynamics, made a similar point almost 30 years ago:

> One often sees in the social science literature assertions that the act of studying an organization, say a corporation, will alert people to questions about their actions and that the study process itself will cause changes in behavior. I do not believe this is true. It is much harder to change the decision-making procedures than we first realized when system dynamics started. Old mental models and decision habits are deeply ingrained. They do not change on the basis of only a logical argument. Early system dynamics analyses were in the "consultant" mode in which the system dynamicist would study a corporation, go away and build a model, and come back with recommendations. Usually these suggestions would be accepted as a logical argument, but would not alter behavior. Under pressure of daily operations, decisions would revert to prior practice.[3]

In the paradigm that Forrester describes, the model that is constructed is utilized by a consultant—an outsider—to develop recommendations. The model itself is never adopted or used by individuals in the company. In fact, these individuals may only be obliquely aware of the computer model which was utilized to reach conclusions. In other situations, a model is developed expressly for a client to use, usually in the form of a software application. In still other situations, a hybrid approach is adopted—the consulting team develops a computer model for use during an engagement and leaves the software with the client at the conclusion of the engagement.

Regardless of the mode in which the model is utilized, there is the initial challenge of convincing model users that the model has value, that its assumptions are reasonable, that the data that is being fed into it is valid, and that the model outputs are reasonable. Even when the model has been suitably validated and conclusions drawn from its use are considered credible, there remains the challenge of getting people to act on those recommendations. A model whose use does not lead to action may be of academic interest but has little practical value.

The first challenge, the buy-in challenge, takes many forms. There are many people who are naturally suspicious of any kind of computer model. For these people, a computer model is a form of deceit, a kind of magic in which a representation of a real phenomenon is subject to manipulation by the man behind the curtain. For these people, models are not to be trusted and they will take any opportunity to undermine and challenge their validity, especially if model results do not align with their beliefs.[4] Some of these challenges are reasonable, while others are not.

The usual way in which the buy-in challenge is addressed is through model verification and validation. These processes are important but they are not foolproof and always leave room for doubt. Ultimately, whether people accept a model as valid will depend on many factors, some under your control and others not, and the best a modeler can do is be as transparent and straightforward as possible in describing the model and the validation process.

The second challenge—convincing people to act on the recommendations of the model—is in many ways much harder than the first challenge, even if people are convinced of the model's validity.[5] This is a problem of change management and despite all that business gurus have said on this subject, it remains stubbornly difficult to overcome. Jagjit Singh says that to see the results of a model lead to change, the modeler must become a passionate advocate.

> Since operations research is by definition the scientific study of processes and methods of work in the field, office, or on the bench in order to increase efficiency, to the extent it does succeed in discovering ways of improvement, it naturally implies a tacit if friendly criticism of the existing state of affairs. Consequently, an operations research worker has to be extremely tactful and cautious in making such criticism when presenting his discovery. Not that we do not want our friends to tell us our faults so that we may reform

ourselves. We only resent that particular stickler for accuracy who actually does so, as Henry James discovered long ago. This is why the first problem of a good operations research worker is how to be that kind of stickler without provoking resentment. To do so one needs to combine, in a manner of speaking, the detachment of an ascetic with the commitment of a partisan. It is true that scientific neutrality and executive involvement do not go together easily. Nevertheless, it is important for an operations research worker to blend the two. The reason is that while for discovering truth he needs to remain disengaged, for its implementation he has to have the fury of an engaged partisan.[6]

I have no doubt that partisan engagement is necessary to see the successful implementation of a model; I am just not sure that it is sufficient. What those sufficient ingredients are, I don't claim to know with certainty. Following the paradigms that I advocate in this book will not guarantee success but will improve your odds, just as obeying the rules of the road does not guarantee that you will not have an accident, but lowers your risk.

## 1.4   Trade-offs in Computer Modeling

For the most part, the models discussed in this book are not highly complex, at least compared to the kinds of computer models scientists use for things like modeling global climate or protein folding. Nonetheless, they require care and thought to build and like any model, their construction involves making trade-offs between model fidelity, usability, and speed of delivery.

The issue of model fidelity is one that arises every time you construct a model. In each of the case studies in this book, I had to decide on the level of detail and scope of the model. These choices are made at every step of the modeling process. Often, the time and budget allocated for the project dictates how detailed the model can be. One might argue that it should be the other way around—the level of detail required should form the basis for determining the timeline and budget. In a world without constraints, this would be the right approach. Unfortunately, in most business contexts, there is often a deadline or a fixed budget that is imposed a priori. We often have no choice but to tailor our solution approach to the constraints imposed by our customers. This extends beyond just timeline and budget constraints. Customer expectations about the capabilities of the model are a key consideration in deciding on model fidelity. If the customer is focused on understanding the trade-off between inventory and service levels, a model that assumes deterministic demand is not likely to be sufficient.

Speed of delivery is a critical component of effective modeling and it trumps model fidelity in most circumstances. Delivery encompasses all aspects of model development and deployment: design, development, testing, verification and validation of the model itself, data collection, cleansing, and processing, and user training and documentation. If model delivery takes too long and consequently the model is not available when needed, it has lost much of its value. A simpler model that can be deployed quickly and is easy to use is much more valuable than a highly complex one that is delivered late and is difficult to use. In every case described in this book and in every model-building project in which I have been involved, speed of delivery has been a critical factor in the success of the project. In cases where the model was not delivered in a timely fashion, its use was compromised.

Model usability is another important consideration that needs to be weighed against fidelity and speed. Usually, the models we build are not intended for large numbers of users. The principal users are in fact sometimes the model builders themselves. Usability is focused not so much on how intuitive the user interface is but on how easy it is to perform the desired kinds of analyses with the model. The kinds of questions relating to usability that a modeler should be thinking about when designing a model include:

- How much effort is involved in defining a scenario within the model?
- Is it easy to compare different scenarios?
- What is the run-time performance of the model? How quickly does the model run?
- Does using the model require users to learn how to use new software?
- Is the model output easy to understand and navigate?
- How difficult is it to refresh the input data to the model?

In general, model usability and fidelity run up against constraints on speed of delivery and budget. There is no simple formula for deciding where on the spectrum of fidelity, speed, and usability a particular project should fall. But the trade-offs should be kept in mind throughout the project.

## 1.5    A Framework for Computer Modeling

A computer model is constructed for a purpose and that purpose should be kept clearly in mind during all phases of development. When developing a model, it is useful to think about its purpose along several dimensions. First are three dimensions that characterize the model itself:

1. Is the model intended primarily for performance evaluation or for optimization?
2. Is the model stochastic or is it deterministic?
3. Is the model dynamic or static?

Along the first dimension, an optimization model is one in which an optimal, or near-optimal, solution to a problem is desired. In a performance evaluation model, the model is designed only to assess performance for a given set of inputs, which completely determine the model outputs. Any optimization model can be utilized for performance evaluation because implicit in optimization is the ability to evaluate any candidate solution. By the same token, a performance evaluation model can be utilized, at least in principle, to perform optimization—an optimization procedure can be created by wrapping an optimization algorithm around the performance evaluation model.

A stochastic model has at least one input specified as a probability distribution and at least one output that is a function of that probability distribution. A stochastic model need not be a simulation model, though that is often the case in practice. Many stochastic models are purely analytical. For example, queueing models and stochastic inventory models are two classes of stochastic models that don't rely on simulation. When I worked at IBM, I helped to develop a stochastic performance evaluation model to predict performance of semiconductor factories using a queueing network model.[7]

The distinction between static and dynamic models is perhaps the least well-defined, at least at the edges. A dynamic model typically varies with time while a static model is one that has no time dimension to it. I think of a dynamic model as one in which the passage of time is explicitly incorporated so that the model output varies as a function of time. A static model may have output that varies but not as a function of time. Often, the static versus dynamic distinction is confused with the stochastic versus deterministic distinction. For the most part, I believe these are orthogonal, independent distinctions. There are stochastic models that are static or dynamic and there are deterministic models that are static or dynamic.

To understand these first three dimensions, it may be helpful to consider some examples.

- A linear program is a deterministic optimization model. It may be static or dynamic, depending on whether the formulation incorporates multiple time periods. As with any optimization model, it can also be used for performance evaluation. It is a trivial matter to take an arbitrary set of values for the decision variables in a linear program and evaluate the objective function and constraints.
- A discrete event simulation is (usually) a stochastic, dynamic, performance evaluation model. There is an inherent time component in a discrete event simulation, so even if the input stochastic distributions are stationary and steady state performance measures are what is of interest, it is still dynamic because of transient, time-dependent behavior.
- A Monte Carlo simulation is a stochastic, static, performance evaluation model. One can introduce the element of time into a Monte Carlo simulation so it is possible for Monte Carlo simulations to be dynamic.
- A global climate model is a dynamic, deterministic, performance evaluation model.
- The economic order quantity model is a static, deterministic, optimization model.

- Most queueing models are static, stochastic, performance evaluations models.
- A linear regression model is a deterministic, static, optimization model. This may raise some eyebrows. While it is true that linear regression typically involves data that has some degree of randomness, the inputs to a regression model do not consist of probability distributions, but merely a matrix of numbers. The purpose of a linear regression model is to find a set of parameters that minimizes the error of the linear model; thus, it is an optimization model. And it is static in that the parameters that define the model do not vary with time. On the other hand, it is not at all unusual for a linear regression model to represent time as a set of dummy variables (for example, month or day of week) or as an explicit variable itself. So, in this sense, some linear regression models can be thought of as dynamic.

There is a second set of dimensions that relate to how the model will be used and should be thought about during the design phase of model development. These include:

1. Is the model intended for one-time use or for repeated, ongoing use?
2. Is the model going to be used by few or many users?
3. Is the model going to be used by a consulting team only or will it be delivered to the client?

Among other things, the answers to these questions will determine how much effort needs to go into developing a user interface. For example, models that are for one-time use by a consulting team will require much less effort than a model that is intended for multiple users on an ongoing basis.

## 1.6   Modeling Paradigms

There are a number of rules of the road that modelers should follow. I include here a summary of modeling paradigms that are illustrated in the case studies to follow. These are general modeling guidelines that may be useful to individuals who are new to model building.

1. **Collect data early and often.** Collecting data is shorthand for the usually time-consuming process of specifying what data is needed to populate a model, identifying sources for the data, writing code to extract data, analyzing the data to identify outliers and assess its validity, and processing the data to transform it into a usable format. This is an iterative process as data requirements evolve during model development and as issues with data quality and data availability surface. The data collection process is almost always the bottleneck in model development. Starting the process early and iterating often is a key to success.

2. **Perform sensitivity analysis.** Performing extensive sensitivity analysis on input values is a good way to increase confidence in model results. Often, sensitivity analysis is the only practical way to deal with model inputs that are either unknown or known only very roughly. If sensitivity analysis shows that modifying a model input results in a significant change in a key output metric, and if that model input is not known precisely, it may be worth investing time and resources to better measure that model input if that is possible. On the other hand, sensitivity analysis often reveals the opposite: that varying an input does not materially affect key output metrics. Providing this insight is critical.

3. **Build the model parsimoniously and iteratively.** The law of diminishing returns as applied to model building, discussed in the last chapter of this book, says that increased model complexity buys you marginally decreasing accuracy. In other words, as more detail is added to a model, its incremental value, measured in terms of increased accuracy and ultimately increased insight, shrinks quickly. A consequence of this law is that one should add detail to a model with great care, recognizing the increased time and cost associated with adding additional detail and estimating the incremental accuracy it will provide. A good approach is to start with a simple model that can be implemented quickly and then add functionality incrementally, even if this results in some duplicated effort or code that is discarded.

Only add complexity when the added complexity is clearly necessary. The benefits are many. Individuals new to modeling often err on the side of including more detail into a model because of the belief that more is better. But more often than not, the advantages of including more detail have not been adequately weighed against their cost. Experienced modelers know that more complex models do not necessarily buy more insight, only more headaches.

4. **Build a prototype instead of a detailed requirements document.** The traditional approach followed in software development is to create a document which describes the functional and non-functional requirements of the software, which is then used by the software architect to design the software. In creating decision models, following this process can be time-consuming and unproductive. Where possible, it is preferable to build a model prototype quickly which can then be used, if necessary, as the basis for a requirements document.

5. **Use general purpose software and freely available software first before turning to more specialized, proprietary tools.** This does not mean developing your own linear programming routines from scratch. It does mean leveraging the considerable quantity of high quality software and software libraries available in the public domain and using standard desktop software to build user interfaces.

6. **Pay attention to run time performance.** The longer a model takes to run, the less likely it will be used. Models that take many hours or days to run a single scenario are going to be used far less often than models that can provide results in seconds or minutes. To some extent, the bane of model builders is software developers who are often more concerned with creating the most elegant software solution rather than the most efficient one.

7. **Separate data from model logic as much as possible**. The idea here, well known among experienced modelers, is to keep the logical specification of the model separate from the data that instantiates the model. There are many benefits of doing so. Many modeling languages explicitly support this paradigm. For example, SIMAN, the underlying language of the simulation product Arena, requires users to separate models into two components, a .mod component which describes the model logic, and a .exp component which contains the data to drive

the model. Another example is AMPL, a modeling environment for linear and integer programming. But many others, unfortunately, do not. In particular, it is difficult, if not impossible, to separate data from model logic when using a spreadsheet tool such as Excel. The model logic in this case is usually embedded in the cell formulas. But all the cells in Excel, whether they contain formulas or data, appear the same, unless the user makes an effort to separate them.

8. **Use variance reduction techniques whenever possible.** Variance reduction techniques are relevant in stochastic models, in particular when performing simulations using pseudo-random numbers. The most widespread example of a variance reduction technique is using common random numbers when running multiple simulations. Using variance reduction techniques, even imperfectly, can lead to dramatically reduced confidence intervals when comparing simulation output across multiple scenarios.

9. **When it comes to optimization, don't let perfect be the enemy of good.** Business decisions that are complex enough to justify building a computer model typically require making trade-offs among multiple competing objectives. In most cases, there is not a single right answer and the computer model that generates only a single "optimal" answer, such as the solution to a linear program, is usually not helpful in getting to a good solution. More often than not, a model that can generate many good solutions, some that perform better along certain criteria and others that perform better along others, is preferable to a model that only outputs a single answer. Also, the computation time required to find a provably optimal solution may be much more than that required to find good solutions, and those good solutions may actually be just as valuable, if not preferable, to the provably optimal solution.

10. **Speed trumps reuse.** Often, the need for a computer model arises when a company is facing a difficult decision and there is urgency to assess different alternatives and develop recommendations on the best course of action. In these cases, the need to rapidly create a useful model trumps the usual protocols of software development. The resulting model will be purpose-built and may not be easily reused for future decisions. That should not be viewed as a defect but as a deliberate choice.

11. **Be transparent.** When describing a model that has been used to reach decisions or make recommendations, be completely transparent about modeling assumptions, limitations, and potential weaknesses. If you try to hide these, you will only succeed in raising suspicions about it. Most people with some sense of what computer modeling is will understand these limitations and will not reject the results because it does not conform exactly to reality. But there will always be people, who for a variety of reasons, ranging from ignorance to self-interest, will raise objections to the model and sow seeds of doubt in people's minds about its efficacy. Often, these people don't believe in the value of computer models or are suspicious of them because they don't understand them. On the other hand, people who object to the use of a computer model may have legitimate concerns. For example, it is often the case that computer models have a number of tuning parameters built in. By varying these parameters, a modeler can often obtain vastly different results. If the setting of these parameters is not done transparently and in a way which can be justified based on reasonable assumptions, people may rightfully feel that the model has been tweaked to obtain the results that the model builder or executive sponsor wants to see.

12. **Models by themselves will not lead to change.** A computer model is a tool and a tool is only useful insofar as people know how and when to use it, and are motivated to use it. Even if people understand the model and accept its assumptions as reasonable, it does not follow that people will embrace its recommendations and change behavior as a result. The model may point the way forward or may provide valuable insight, but it is individuals who must how figure out how to leverage the tool so that it leads to positive, sustained change. Often, the only way to effect real change in an organization is to change incentives.

## 1.7    Summary of Case Studies

The case studies in Chapters 2 to 9 of this book cover a wide range of different topics and are presented in no particular order. Some end happily, meaning the models developed were built and utilized successfully.

Others do not and are offered not as discouraging but as cautionary tales, and to point out the ways in which things can go wrong. Still others fall somewhere in between—the modeling effort had limited success but could have been more successful. I am a firm believer in learning from mistakes and the cases that did not turn out as well as desired I think have as much to teach, if not more, than their more successful brethren. A brief synopsis of each case follows.

Chapter 2: This chapter describes an analysis of a plant expansion opportunity using a simple static, deterministic, performance evaluation model on top of which was layered a high level probabilistic assessment. The client requested that its name not be used and for the industry in which it operates to be masked.

Chapter 3: This chapter deals with understanding the impact of scheduling in semiconductor manufacturing. It reports on work I carried out with colleagues over several years when I worked at IBM. The work leveraged several different models: a discrete event simulation, a scheduling model based on a fluid network model, and some purely mathematical models (whose results provided some insight into results we observed).

Chapter 4: This chapter describes a distribution network rationalization project which utilized a static, deterministic, optimization model to identify opportunities for reducing operating costs and working capital. An interesting challenge in this work was to capture inventory costs in a credible way.

Chapter 5: This chapter describes utilizing a discrete event simulation to identify opportunities for inventory and cycle time reductions at a specialty steel manufacturer—a good example of a case in which the model was successfully designed, built and tested but the data necessary to make it useful was never fully collected and validated. I take the opportunity in this case to lay out the argument for building a discrete event simulation from scratch in a general purpose programming language, rather than utilizing commercial software packages. These latter definitely have their place, especially if you are interested in animation, but they come at a cost.

Chapter 6: This chapter is about a goal programming solution to a distribution planning problem for a musical instrument rental company.

A mostly successful case with some difficult patches related to the use of third party software.

Chapter 7: This chapter differs from others in this book in that it talks about the fundamental limitations of a commercial supply chain planning software solution that I worked with at i2 Technologies. I think it is an interesting cautionary tale of how a commercial software modeling tool fails because it lacks a crucial ingredient, the ability to formulate and solve the very problems that the software is intended to address.

Chapter 8: This chapter is about calculating price elasticity curves for a tourism company. This case reports on a short, successful project that utilized regression models to estimate price elasticities for packaged vacations. A challenging aspect of this work was thinking through in an iterative manner how to deal with a variety of confounding factors.

Chapter 9: This chapter describes using a discrete event simulation to improve the throughput of a truck manufacturing facility. The case illustrates the point that variability—in this case, in the form of random failures of machinery—can dramatically affect the performance of a system.

## Endnotes

1. See, for example, Kaner and Bach (2002) and Whittaker, J., Arbon, J., and Carollo, J. (2012).
2. The currently popular agile development philosophy abbreviates or eliminates many of the steps that have traditionally been followed in software development.
3. Forrester (1989).
4. As an obvious example, I need hardly mention the legions of climate science deniers who view global climate models in this vein.
5. It is exactly akin to the challenge of getting people to substantially change their behavior to reduce man-made carbon emissions even if the vast majority of humanity accepts GCM projections that this is necessary to avoid the worst effects of global warming.
6. Singh (1968).
7. See Connors, Feigin, and Yao (1996).

# CHAPTER 2

# Assessing Risk and Opportunities of a Manufacturing Plant Expansion

Major strategic decisions for many companies are often fraught with uncertainty. If we build a new manufacturing plant, will demand for the products it produces be adequate to justify its construction? What might competitors do that would affect the outcome? Will our customers stay with us or will they find alternative suppliers? Will there be adequate supplies to feed the new factory? In these situations, we find ourselves coping with uncertainty, not risk, a distinction that the economist Frank Knight made in 1921.[1] James Surowiecki characterized Knight's distinction as follows:

> Risk . . . is something you can calculate—the probability of someone losing at roulette. Uncertainty, though, arises when the odds of success or failure are incalculable—the probability of someone deciding to play roulette in the first place, and being pickpocketed on the way out of the casino.[2]

In modeling, we tend to focus on measurable risk—those situations in which we can assign a probability distribution to events. And we tend to shy away from uncertainty—those situations in which, like the player who decides to play roulette and is pick-pocketed on the way out, the assignment of probabilities seems hopeless. And yet, many of the kinds of decisions that companies routinely wrestle with, especially strategic decisions, involve this kind of uncertainty. Can modeling help in these circumstances? I think it can.

Some time ago, the CEO of one of the world's major producers of chorg,[3] a key ingredient in a large range of consumer products, approached us about helping the company decide whether to invest in a new technology that would significantly expand the supply of glog, the key raw material for chorg production. The investment in question was to build a new plant, at significant expense, to produce glog using this new technology. The advantage of the new technology, compared to standard methods of producing glog, was that it resulted in a higher quality glog, especially for blue glog, which was considered, prior to the advent of this new technology, inferior to red and yellow glog. The new technology was proven so there was no risk that it might not work when scaled to industrial production. Also, the decision on where to locate the plant was already determined because it needed to be co-located with a large processing facility where the supply of blue glog precursor would be plentiful. But there were a host of other uncertainties that made the decision to build the new plant not at all clear-cut.

Ultimately, the decision on whether to build the plant rested on how the commodity price for glog would evolve over time. If the price declined so that it was below the cost of the new factory to produce it and stayed there for a significant period of time, the plant would not be viable. If the price remained stable or rose, it would be profitable and the payback would be appealing. But many factors could affect the price of glog and how these factors played out over time was going to dictate whether the investment would be viewed in hindsight as a wise one. Unfortunately, hindsight was not a luxury the CEO could rely on. A decision was needed quickly on whether to move forward with plant construction or not.

When we got involved with the process, we had approximately eight weeks in which to help the team, which was tasked with making a recommendation on whether to proceed with building the plant or not, to think through the decision and the factors that affected it. So, any model we could develop in that time frame would of necessity be put together quickly and roughly. We argued from the outset that we could not build a credible model that would predict the price of glog. We viewed this as a hopeless task in the time frame we had and with the information at our disposal. (Even if we had more time, building a predictive model for the price of a commodity was a fool's errand.) But we proposed that we could build a model that would allow the company to look at different scenarios affecting supply and demand for glog. By looking at a range of scenarios and identifying those which would likely put the investment decision at risk, we could help clarify which specific combinations of factors would lead to negative outcomes, if any. On top of that, we could layer a qualitative risk assessment in which we judged the likelihood of each scenario occurring. This likelihood would not be probabilistically precise because it involved an assessment of uncertain events for which exact probabilities could not realistically be assigned. But it would provide a relative view of risk—for example, whether a given scenario was likely or not to occur—which was the best we could hope to do given the enormous uncertainties involved.

We grouped factors that would affect supply and demand of glog into three broad categories: competitor actions, market shifts, and environmental effects. Among competitor actions were a range of possible outcomes ranging from competitors not making any significant changes to their production to significant plants coming online that would increase the supply of glog and chorg. Market shifts included three major factors: higher or lower chorg market growth, more or less processed glog precursor (which would affect the availability of glog), and growth of alternative chorg sources, including alpha chorg, which came from another raw material. Environmental effects included the impact of flactation (a serious bacterial infection) on red glog supply, the possibility of long-term drought in South Africa and its impact on the yellow glog precursor raw material there, and the overall likelihood of sustained growth or decline in worldwide glog precursor production.

In addition to these largely exogenous factors, we needed to layer in possible mitigating responses on the part of the company in reaction to potential negative outcomes. These responses included: shedding of contractual commitments to buy glog from suppliers if there was a sustained excess supply of glog, running the new glog plant at lower than full capacity, increasing the capacity of their existing chorg production plants, increasing the quantity of glog inventory held, and converting the new glog plant into a chorg plant.

The model we constructed was a deterministic model that captured the world-wide chorg supply chain from raw material to final product over 10 years in yearly increments. It allowed users to set key assumptions about the effects of exogenous factors and mitigating responses, and view the impact of these assumptions played out over 10 years on glog demand and supply, glog year-ending inventory, chorg demand and supply, and chorg year-ending inventory.

We used the model to evaluate hundreds of different scenarios. Each scenario was assessed on the basis of two criteria: its favorability to the investment project, and its likelihood of occurring. To simplify, we decided that each criteria would be assessed at one of two levels: high and low. This provided an easy to digest 2 x 2 matrix for characterizing each scenario. We debated whether increasing the complexity of assessment of each criteria or of adding additional criteria made sense and though there were arguments in favor, we ultimately decided that in order to ease the process of communicating our results throughout the company, we should err on the side of keeping the assessment criteria fairly simple for an already complicated decision process.

Working through this process, we found no scenarios in which the plant was built that fell into the quadrant of high likelihood of occurring and low favorability to the project. This was surprising but we probed some of the low favorability scenarios and convinced everyone involved that these were in fact low-likelihood outcomes.

One interesting finding that became a key part of the story was that there were a large number of scenarios in which the plant was not built which were viewed as high risk to the company, because the supply of glog in those scenarios became highly constrained. This risked choking the entire supply chain for chorg, which would jeopardize the company's business. As a result of these scenarios, many of which were judged likely to occur, we came to the conclusion that not building the new glog plant was in many respects a higher risk strategy than building it. This only became apparent after looking at a large number of scenarios and would probably not have emerged so clearly had the modeling effort not been undertaken.

At the board of directors meeting at which our recommendations were presented, I was asked how we arrived at assessing the likelihood of a given scenario occurring. I could not claim that there was any scientific precision involved. The likelihood of a competitor building a glog plant, of a significant increase in flactation disease of glog precursor in California, of Cuba vastly increasing its production of alpha chorg, or of some combination of these three events falls squarely in the domain of uncertainty, not risk; to assign specific probabilities to these events is an exercise in false precision. Instead, I simply said that we, as a team, judged the likelihood of the scenarios based on our collective knowledge and experience, which was the best that we could do.

The plant is now under construction.

## Endnotes

1. Knight (1921).
2. Surowiecki (2003).
3. Names and places have been masked at the request of the client. Chorg, glog, glog precursor, and flactation are made up names.

# CHAPTER 3

# Scheduling Semiconductor Fabs

The mass production of computer chips in commercial semiconductor fabrication facilities is one of the most impressive engineering feats of modern times. In a fab, silicon wafers undergo a series of etching operations to imprint circuits on the silicon. A single wafer typically contains hundreds or thousands of individual chips, often, but not always, identical. Each chip is composed of millions of individual transistors. After processing in the fab, the wafers are cut into individual chips and each chip packaged into a finished product.

When I was starting out my career in the research division at IBM, I focused on scheduling of semiconductor fabs. Wafers circulate in a fab in lots, each of which contains a dozen or so individual wafers. Each lot visits a sequence of work centers to have various operations performed related to circuit etching: deposition, material removal, photolithography, chemical property modification, etc. The number of discrete operations that each wafer undergoes before completion and the number of distinct work centers in a fab depend on chip complexity. Typically, the number of operations to produce a semiconductor chip in a current commercial fab is in the order of 1000, performed at approximately 100 distinct work centers.

Many of these operations are performed at the same work centers because the construction of a chip requires layering a series of circuits on top of each other and each layer requires roughly the same set of operations to create. So, for example, the photolithography work center might be visited 10 times by the same lot during its processing, each time undergoing a different operation.

The phenomenon of wafer lots periodically returning to the same work center during the course of processing is known as "re-entrant flow" and it presents logistical challenges to those responsible for managing a fab. At any given time, thousands of lots may be circulating in a commercial fab, all at different stages of production and all competing for access to the same work centers. Coupled with re-entrant flow, this means that whenever a work center becomes free to begin work on a new lot, there may be several lots in different stages of processing in queue at the work station that are waiting to be processed there. The scheduling challenge is this: How does one select among the lots waiting to be processed at a work center which one to process next?

At the time that I was focused on this problem in the 1990s, this was a popular area of research in operations research and industrial engineering. Because the capital required to build a fab is enormous (upwards of $2B to construct a state-of-the-art fab today), management is understandably focused on maximizing asset utilization. That means doing everything possible to keep bottleneck work centers in the fab utilized and not starved of work. It also means trying to maximize the throughput of the factory. Both of these objectives are reasonable (although producing chips for which there is no demand simply to maximize factory utilization is problematic) but the challenge is in understanding the connection between these objectives and the logistical decisions made each time a work center becomes free.

Plant managers have a lot to worry about and the first question any manager should ask in response to this problem is: Does it matter? In other words, is this a problem a plant manager should be worrying about or is following a simple queueing discipline like *first-come-first-served* going to perform about as well as any other discipline? At the time, the answer to this question was not known, but a common belief was that scheduling was important and could have a big impact on fab performance. Even a small impact could be viewed as significant if, for example, it resulted in bottleneck work station utilization increasing by a few percent. As a result, many researchers proposed a variety of different scheduling disciplines intended to outperform others. The problem was that there was no easy way to test different scheduling disciplines on actual semiconductor lines. Plant managers were understandably reluctant to have their fabs serve as guinea pigs, given the large stakes.

At first glance, it might not be apparent how many different kinds of scheduling disciplines there are. One can differentiate among lots at a work center in many ways: the type of chips in the lot, where in its processing sequence it is, the number of wafers in it, its due date for completion (based on customer commitment), etc. Scheduling policies can utilize any differentiating factors among lots as well as information about the state of the factory to decide which lot to select next at a work center. The proposed methods vary from the extremely simple to the arcane. At the simple end of the spectrum are completely local policies like *first-come-first-served* (process lots in the sequence in which they arrive to the work center), *shortest-processing-time-first* (process lots that have the shortest expected processing time at the work center first) and *earliest-due-date* (process the lot that has been promised to be complete soonest). These are considered local policies because they rely only on information pertaining to the lots awaiting process at the work center or to the work center itself. More complex policies look at information beyond the current work center. For example, policies such as *closest to completion* (select the lot that has the least amount of time remaining to complete production) and *least slack* (select the lot that is trailing most behind its due date) depend on where the lot is in its processing and how much additional processing is required. These policies have variants depending on how you measure time remaining: number of operations remaining, amount of processing time remaining, expected cycle time remaining (including processing plus queueing time). More complex policies solve optimization problems to determine which lot to process next. For example, together with my colleagues Dan Connors and David Yao, I proposed a scheduling policy based on a fluid network model of a fab, which involved solving a sequence of linear programs.[1]

There are also complications that arise when scheduling work centers that process lots in batches. The rules for batching are often complex and may limit which lots can be combined with others in a batch. A goal at a batch processing work center may be to fill a batch as much as possible, which may conflict with other scheduling objectives. Resolving these conflicting objectives is non-trivial.

Without access to fabs to test scheduling policies and measure their performance, researchers have two choices: (1) attempt to prove mathematically that their policy performs optimally according to some metric under some prescribed circumstances; or (2) build an accurate simulation model of the fab and test the policies using this model. The problem with the first choice is that establishing optimality or near optimality in a mathematical sense almost always requires making assumptions about the system that are vastly more simplistic than those that obtain in a real fab. The optimality results are therefore not necessarily applicable to an actual fab.

The second approach of building a simulation of the fab is a more robust approach than the first but it is time-consuming both to construct the model and to collect the data to populate it. At first, when we started the scheduling research at IBM, we were encouraged by the fact that in order to test our policies, we would not have to start from scratch in building a simulation model; IBM already had built a detailed discrete event simulation of several of their fabs. The simulation model had been constructed over several years and had been extensively validated. The simulation model was put at our disposal so we naively believed it would be a simple matter of leveraging it to test different scheduling policies. Nothing was further from the truth.

It turned out that when the simulation was written, no one considered that people might be interested in using the simulation to test scheduling policies. As a result, the simulation model was constructed with the hard-coded assumption that lots at a work center would be processed in the *first-come-first-served* discipline. To change the logic of the simulation was not a simple undertaking. After much investment of time and effort, we modified the simulation so that the scheduling discipline could be altered. The problem still remained that implementing anything but the simplest disciplines required a considerable effort to code and debug. For example, to test the fluid network policy required that at periodic intervals during the course of a simulation run, the simulation code needed to be interrupted to call a separate piece of code that would recalculate queueing priorities at each work center. These would then be fed back to the simulation which then continued to run.

The other problem we faced was related to run-time performance. The simulation code was extremely complex and was written with little focus on run-time efficiency. The end result in this situation was that a single simulation of a realistic sized fab for one year required one to two days to run.

The long waits to perform each simulation hampered our ability to analyze scheduling policies. Often, we would set a simulation running and after looking at the results a few days later, we would realize some basic mistake had been made and we would need to re-run the simulation. It was a painfully long and arduous process to test the policies we were interested in comparing. Even when we had completed testing, we were left with the nagging feeling that some of the more complex policies may not have been implemented correctly in the simulation because they did not perform as well as we expected. Was it that the complex policies were in fact no better than the simpler policies or was it that they were incorrectly implemented in the simulation? We never answered this question to our complete satisfaction.

Having said that, the results obtained after much testing revealed a negative conclusion, namely that the work center scheduling policy did not significantly affect overall fab performance as measured by throughput, cycle time, and work center utilization. The policies did affect the performance of specific lots if they were given priority over other lots, which is not at all surprising. But the bottom line seemed to be that there is no free lunch: priority given to one set of lots is at the expense of others that are forced to wait.

That is not to say that one cannot construct deliberately bad scheduling policies, which systematically attempt to starve bottleneck machines and cause system throughput to degrade. But excluding such pathological policies, which one has to work hard at devising, the chief conclusion from our work was that overall fab performance could not be significantly changed by varying the work center scheduling policy. That does not mean that scheduling policies are not important, just that their importance lies elsewhere. For example, it may be quite important to the plant manager to achieve on-time delivery of certain lots. By prioritizing these lots, scheduling policies can improve their on-time delivery performance. But don't ask for the impossible—a scheduling policy cannot improve on-time delivery performance uniformly for all lots.

## 3.1    Some Insights from Mathematics Models of Scheduling

The mathematical results proven about scheduling policies have been established in the context of queueing systems. Even if these results apply only to fairly simple queueing networks that don't approximate the complexity of a wafer fab, they are consistent with the results we found when testing scheduling policies in fabs. These mathematical models give insight as to why the scheduling policies don't seem to have a major impact on overall fab performance.

The simplest possible system in which to study the impact of scheduling discipline on performance is a single server queue processing a single class of customers. Think of an ATM with a queue of customers waiting to perform transactions. If we assume that we don't know in advance exactly how long each customer will require to be processed, but that the expected processing time of all customers is the same, it turns out that the most interesting result proven to date about such a simple system is in fact a negative result: as far as the average waiting time is concerned, the queueing discipline has no effect. That is, regardless of what scheduling policy is followed, the average waiting time remains the same. The only impact queueing discipline has on waiting times is on higher order moments. It has been proven that among all scheduling policies, *first-come-first-served* minimizes waiting time variance while *last-come-first-served* maximizes waiting time variance. All other scheduling policies fall somewhere in between. In some sense, this confirms our intuition that *first-come-first-served* discipline is the fairest. On the other hand, when we know something about the processing time of customers and can differentiate customers in queue based on their processing time, this result does not hold, as anyone who has been in a supermarket check-out line can attest to. In these situations, giving priority to shorter processing time customers can lower overall wait time. This explains the motivation for using a *shortest-processing-time-first* discipline.

Similar mathematical results have been proven for more complex systems with multiple customer classes. A customer class in this context means customers that can be grouped together because they have the same *expected* processing times.[2] These results establish that the work in certain types of queueing networks remains invariant as a function of scheduling policy, assuming that the scheduling policies are non-idling, meaning they never deliberately keep a server idle when a customer is present waiting to be served.[3] What we mean by work in the system at any given moment is the amount of time required to process all customers in the system, assuming no other customers arrive to the system. The average work in the system does not exactly correspond to average customer waiting times but work is a close surrogate for waiting time and in some special cases, average work in system can be shown to be equal to average waiting time. In these situations, the results prove that scheduling policies don't have any effect on average waiting times across all customer classes. In other words, if we take a straight average of waiting times across all customers, this average will be the same regardless of the scheduling discipline followed. What this implies is that a scheduling policy that gives priority to one set of customers over another will reduce the waiting times of the higher priority customers but at the same time will increase the waiting times of the lower priority customers. And this will happen in such a way that the overall average waiting time does not change. These results suggest that scheduling rules will not significantly alter overall system performance when viewed in aggregate, which is consistent with our fab simulation empirical tests.

This is a good example of a situation in which a theoretical mathematical model can provide significant insight into the operation of a complex real-world system, even if the modeling assumptions are violated in the real-world system. There are many people even today who argue that scheduling of jobs in a factory is critically important to the overall performance of the factory. They would argue that these theoretical results don't apply because their assumptions are not valid. But the evidence from our work is that they do seem to apply. So, who is right? My advice to a plant manager would be to insist on proof in the form of a simulation that demonstrates the efficacy of any proposed scheduling policy.

## 3.2   Lot Release Policies

Another conclusion we found—again, not at all surprising—is that the *lot release* policy (the policy for deciding when to release lots into the factory) has a much greater impact on overall fab performance than the scheduling policy. For the plant manager concerned foremost with overall fab performance, paying attention to the lot release policy is much more critical than the scheduling policy. Why? Because the lot release policy directly controls how many lots are circulating in the factory. And controlling how many lots are circulating in the factory turns out to be much more important than the order in which lots are processed at work centers from the perspective of overall fab performance, precisely because the lot release policy directly affects the amount of work in the system, which relates directly to fab performance objectives of equipment utilization, throughput, and cycle times.

One might imagine that if the objective is to maximize throughput of the fab or to ensure that bottleneck work centers are never starved for work, a reasonable lot release policy would be to flood the fab with lots, thus ensuring that there is always work available at work centers. The problem with this approach is two-fold. First, by introducing more WIP into the system, the average cycle time of individual lots increases.[4] Thus, the more lots that are circulating, the longer the average production lead time is. Second, as more WIP is introduced to the system, a point is reached where throughput actually starts to degrade, which may not seem intuitively obvious. This occurs because a fab, like any factory, has a limited amount of buffer space where lots can be stored. As this buffer space becomes more and more full, the likelihood of blockages and congestion occurring at the buffer storage areas when retrieving or putting away lots increases. This is an incipient form of deadlock, a theoretical phenomenon which occurs when all the buffer locations become full and no production can occur because completed lots cannot exit work centers. In a real manufacturing system, deadlock does not occur (one can always find a bit of extra space to store a lot in a fab) but congestion can and does slow the rate of production.

On the other hand, a lot release policy that overly limits the amount of WIP in the system can cause starvation of bottleneck work centers and lower factory throughput. So there is a natural tension between limiting the release of lots into the fab and thereby preventing congestion and flooding the fab with work, and thereby keeping work centers busy. Effective lot release policies allow plant managers to find the right balance between these two forces. One such family of policies are constant WIP (conwip) policies, which aim to keep the WIP in a factory at a constant level. Many other lot release policies have been proposed. The debate continues on what the best lot release policy for wafer fabs is.

# Endnotes

1. Connors, Feigin, and Yao (1994).
2. This does not mean that customers in the same class have the same processing times, just that they all have statistically the same processing time requirements (i.e. have the same processing time distribution).
3. See, for example, Federgruen and Groenevelt (1988) and Shanthikumar and Yao (1992).
4. This is a consequence of Little's Law, which states that the average WIP in a system equals the average time that an entity spends in the system times the average rate at which entities enter the system.

# CHAPTER 4

# Rationalizing a Distribution Network for a Chemical Distributor

## 4.1 Problem Motivation

A common problem that many companies struggle with is determining the right physical infrastructure to support their businesses. How many factories and distribution centers should be there, where they should be located, how big they should be, what products should be sourced from which factories, how distribution centers should be replenished, and how customer orders should be fulfilled, are some questions to be answered. Often, these kinds of questions lie dormant for long periods until some trigger event occurs that brings urgency to the matter. It may be that the company is outgrowing its existing manufacturing and distribution footprint and needs to expand its capacity. Or it may be that the business is shrinking and there may be opportunities to reduce costs by consolidating physical infrastructure. Or it may be that the company has gone through a series of acquisitions and is trying to rationalize the disparate assets from those acquisitions.

Whatever the situation, the approach a company takes to answer these questions depends a great deal on the circumstances and the people involved. One common approach is to build a business case around a particular expansion or consolidation opportunity. The business case lays out the assumptions around the opportunity, assesses the capital and operational costs associated with it, and derives investment metrics such as payback period and internal rate of return. Building a business case is a reasonable approach if the possible opportunities that one wants to examine are limited to a small number, say, something less than five. As the number of possibilities rises above this, a point is quickly reached where the manual construction of business models for every opportunity becomes too difficult and time-consuming. An alternative approach is needed, one where searching through large numbers of possible opportunities to find the best solution, or at least viable good solutions, is done in an automated fashion. These kinds of models are generally referred to as network optimization models.

Building a network optimization model is a major undertaking and the decision to build one should not be taken lightly. There are four major pieces involved in the creation of a network optimization model. First, there is the formulation of the model itself, in which the cost and operational elements, level of granularity, decision variables and scope of the model are specified. Second, there is the collection of data to instantiate the model. When you are looking at changes to the physical infrastructure of a supply chain, the data that is required to characterize how the modified supply chain will operate as well as the costs necessary to make the infrastructure changes do not typically exist and need to be collected from scratch, either from external or internal sources. This is always a painful and time-consuming process. Third, there is the development of a solution approach, which is the technique that is going to be applied to find optimal or desirable solutions among all the candidate solutions. And fourth, there is the development of a user interface that allows people to use the model.

When building a network optimization model, there is the usual make or buy decision. Many software companies sell off-the-shelf network optimization packages.[1] Having worked closely with several of these packages over the years, I will say that I am not a big fan of them. For what they provide, they are expensive and they have several limitations that, taken together, usually give me reason enough to opt for the alternative of building a model from scratch.

First, each package has an implicit model formulation that locks you into a level of detail and a cost structure that may not be appropriate for the kind of analysis that you want to do. Second, the software does little to streamline or ease the process of data collection, arguably the most time-consuming and challenging aspect of model development. In fact, because the software typically assumes that data will be provided in a specific format, substantial effort may be necessary to transform raw data into the format required by the software.

Third, the built-in solvers for these packages often have significant limitations in terms of their ability to find solutions in a timely fashion. In its most general form, the underlying mathematical problem that these solutions all need to tackle is a non-linear combinatorial stochastic optimization problem. The non-linearity arises from the fact that some costs—for example, for fixed and semi-variable operating costs—are non-linear functions of the decision variables. The combinatorial aspect arises from the numerous fixed costs associated with infrastructure investments. The stochastic element arises from assessing risks associated with a network configuration, for example, the quantity of safety stock inventory needed to meet a target customer service level. These kinds of problems fall into a class of problems known as NP-hard and finding solutions for them become increasingly difficult as the number of variables and constraints increase. In fact, even for moderate-sized problems that would typically arise for a medium-sized company, finding an optimal solution is effectively impossible on today's computing platforms.

So the developers of these solutions have two choices, neither of them very appealing. They can either force you, through their model formulation, to limit the size and complexity of the problem you can specify so that no problem that you can formulate with the software is unsolvable by the software. At least two packages which I am familiar with do not allow users to incorporate non-linear costs into the problem formulation, effectively forcing users to accept a linear cost model, which is highly unrealistic in many situations. Or they can implement heuristic solvers that are designed to find good solutions but not necessarily optimal ones. The problem with these heuristics is that they tend to be very problem-specific, meaning that they tend to work well for some problems and not well at all for others. It is very hard to create robust heuristics for generic problems.

Because of these limitations, I believe a better approach in most cases is to construct a purpose-built model from scratch, leveraging the extensive software available for free or at a nominal cost to build the solution. Building a model from scratch requires having software and modeling skills in-house or hiring consultants to do the work for you. But if you have the skills, building a bespoke model is not difficult. Model formulation is extremely efficient with the aid of software modeling tools and standard productivity software. Solvers of various types—for linear and mixed integer programming, for instance—are widely available, and for a fraction of the cost of these packaged software solutions. Writing heuristics to solve problems if the solvers don't work is generally much easier for a specific problem formulation than trying to write a generic heuristic. And finally, developing a basic but effective user interface using a combination of Excel and other desktop software can be done quickly and inexpensively.

An important point to keep in mind is that the kinds of problems that network optimization models are designed to solve usually arise infrequently within a company, maybe once every couple of years. Therefore, the models that get developed tend to be for one-time use. In such situations, the benefits and cost savings of constructing the model specifically for your needs make this choice particularly compelling.

## 4.2   Background

A few years ago, I was engaged in a project with a large domestic distributor of chemicals. The company had grown over the years through a combination of organic growth and acquisitions. It had more than 100 storage locations in the U.S. These sites varied from large warehouses that stocked many different products and served multiple customers to small, specialized storage locations that stocked only a few products and served only one or two customers. There were locations that stored liquid chemicals and others that stored dry chemicals. There were special clean areas for storing food-grade chemicals and refrigerated sections for storing products subject to spoilage.

The company had hired us to perform an independent assessment of the opportunity for cost savings by consolidating their warehouses. They wanted us to create a model that would allow us to evaluate different network configurations and to identify an ideal lowest-cost network configuration. As the project progressed, the client made it clear that the top priority was to be able to identify a theoretical lowest-cost network if we were to design a distribution network from the ground up, without re-gard to existing facilities. They referred to this as the "aspirational" model: what the best case solution would look like if they were not tied to exist-ing infrastructure. They knew that this would not be achievable for a va-riety of reasons but they wanted to understand what the upper bound on potential cost savings would be. In coming up with this ideal network, we were instructed to consider any possible locations for distribution centers; we were asked not to restrict attention to where the existing distribution centers were located.

Some people on the team argued that the value of such an aspirational model is quite limited. The model tells you little about what the practi-cal best solution for the company would look like, which everyone knew would be a consolidation to a subset of existing warehouses. And many practical constraints, such as environmental regulations and land-use lim-itations, would prevent expansion of some sites and closure of other sites. Was a solution that could not be implemented really a useful solution at all? Wouldn't it be more useful for us to focus on assessing the potential cost savings through consolidation given the practical constraints that the company faced that limited consolidation and expansion options?

I quickly realized that the model we were to construct needed to an-swer both these questions: (1) What would be the ideal best network configuration without regard to current constraints, and (2) What would be the best configuration taking current constraints into consideration. And further, the model would need to be flexible by being able to fix certain parts of the network and allowing other portions to be optimized, because as soon as the aspirational questions were answered, would come questions about what the practical answer should look like.

## 4.3   Model Design and Formulation

When you think about building a model to address the aspirational question that our client had posed, you realize quickly that you have a challenging problem to tackle. Just compiling the data for the list of candidate sites is daunting. Consider that if you really want to look at all possible locations for warehouses and do this in a realistic manner, you would need to compile a list of all candidate warehouse locations in the US, estimate the costs for leasing or acquiring warehouses at those locations, figure out the environmental, logistical, and operating constraints and costs associated with each location, understand the potential storage capacity of each location, etc.

To get an idea of the difficulty of data collection, let's assume that candidate warehouse locations could be found in, say, 50 percent of all 5-digit zip codes in the US, that is, roughly 20,000 locations. This is a gross understatement of actual candidate locations because there may be multiple warehouse sites within any 5-digit zip code. But for the sake of argument, let us assume only one candidate location per 5-digit zip code.

You first need to gather data on leasing or purchasing a warehouse in each one of these 20,000 locations. Don't forget about environmental regulations and land-use restrictions that might prevent you from operating a chemical distribution facility on the sites. Determine whether there is rail access to the sites and whether tractor trailers are allowed on neighboring roads.

But don't stop there. Now, collect data on the demand for products. As a starting point, use the sales of products to existing customers over the last year. For us, this data was easy enough to extract from the company's Enterprise Resource Planning (ERP) system. There were around 20,000 active stock-keeping units (SKUs) with about 10,000 distinct customer ship-to addresses. The problem is that we don't want to base our desired distribution network on past sales but on anticipated future sales. So we need to generate demand projections for the next five years based on this data.

Next, collect logistics and transportation data. For every SKU, determine the cost to ship from every candidate warehouse to every customer location that has demand for it. If multiple modes are possible—rail, truck, barge—specify costs for each option. Make sure costs are given for full container and less-than-full-container rates. Determine shipment time for each lane. Also, collect inbound shipment costs and times for all products from vendor locations to all candidate warehouses.

Finally, collect data on each SKU: minimum order quantities from vendors, product mass and volumetric measurements to understand storage requirements as a function of volume, storage restrictions, etc.

You will not be finished with these tasks in your lifetime. We had approximately three months with a team of four people to do this. To get anywhere, we knew we would have to simplify the problem while trying to retain the fundamental trade-offs in our problem formulation. This challenge of simplifying but keeping the formulation rich enough to capture key trade-offs is present in one form or another in all modeling work.

As we began to design the model, we had to resolve a number of design questions, the answers to which would determine the data that we would need to populate the model, its capabilities, and the time and effort required to build it. These included the following:

1.  What is the level of detail at which the different components of the distribution network are to be captured? When we started the project, we intended to capture the distribution network at a highly detailed level. We would represent products at the individual SKU level rather than at an aggregate product level, we would represent customers at an individual customer-location level, and we would capture the costs and capabilities of each warehouse at a level commensurate with their financial accounting models. It soon became clear, however, that such a detailed model was going to take far too long to construct. A certain degree of aggregation was going to be necessary in order to complete the project in the desired time frame. We agreed that the right level of aggregation was not at the individual SKU level, where different packaging options gave rise to a huge variety of different products, but at one level above the SKU level, at which packaging differences were ignored.

2.  What is the time scale for the analysis? We agreed that we would look at the costs of operating the supply chain over a one year period. The model would be a single period, static, model and we would get a handle on the impact of demand growth over time on costs by looking at different demand scenarios. All else being equal, higher demand might justify the need for more warehouses, so it was important to understand the sensitivity of the optimal network configuration with respect to product demand.

3.  What is the scope of the network? From a market perspective, we agreed to focus on all U.S. demand and all products. From a supply chain perspective, we agreed that the model would not include

supplier locations but just focus on costs downstream from supplier locations, starting with inbound transportation costs to the warehouses.

4. What are the major cost elements to be captured in the model? At a high level, we agreed that the major costs to include were fixed and variable ongoing operating costs associated with each warehouse in the network, inbound transportation costs, outbound transportation costs, and inventory holding costs.

5. What are the principal performance measures to evaluate a given network configuration? We would focus on the total annual operating costs for the network including inventory holding costs. In addition, we would look at certain service-level implications of a given network configuration, including the percentage of demand that could be satisfied within 24 hours.

Our first challenge was to find a representation of the client's distribution network that would capture all of the relevant costs and constraints of operating the network at a sufficient level of detail that all the project sponsors would view as credible. For fixed costs of operating a warehouse, we decided that to keep things simple at first, we would assume that there is only one fixed cost per warehouse that covers the entire fixed cost for operating the warehouse, assuming a given square footage. A more realistic model would allow step-wise increasing fixed costs as a function of warehouse size. An even more realistic model would allow different fixed costs depending on the type of products that could be handled at the site: a fixed cost for handling dry non-food-grade chemicals, another for liquid chemicals, yet another for refrigerated products, etc. We felt that if a more detailed model for fixed costs was needed, we could incorporate that later.

For variable costs, we assumed that there was a cost per kilogram for each product that passed through a warehouse. Included in this cost would be the put-away, retrieval, staging, and loading/unloading costs. For existing sites, this information could be estimated from the company's accounting systems. For non-existing sites, we assumed that these costs would be comparable to the nearest existing company site.

As for inbound and outbound transportation costs, we agreed to simplify our cost calculations by assuming that they are a linear function of the annual volume on each lane. Also, we would estimate the cost of freight as a linear function of the miles required to drive between two points. Because there are relatively inexpensive applications to estimate truck driving distances and costs between any two locations in the U.S,[2] this gave us a relatively easy way to calculate the transportation cost matrix that would be needed for our model.

For inventory holding costs, we would need to capture the approximate inventory necessary to be held at each distribution center for a given network configuration. The principal drivers of inventory at a distribution center are cycle stock and safety stock. Cycle stock arises when inventory is acquired in larger quantities and is sold in smaller quantities. This may occur if vendors impose minimum order quantities, if discounts are offered on larger purchase quantities, or to reduce inbound transportation costs by, for example, ordering in full truck load quantities. Safety stock is needed to protect against variability in demand and supply and is held in order to provide a certain service level to customers. To simplify the mathematics of the network model, it would be convenient if the inventory required at a warehouse could be approximated as a linear function of the quantity of product flowing through the warehouse. Unfortunately, that is a poor approximation because it ignores minimum order quantity restrictions and risk pooling effects, both of which are non-linear.

To understand the impact of minimum order quantity restrictions on inventory, consider one product with two alternative distribution networks: one consisting of a single distribution center that serves two markets and the other consisting of two distribution centers, each serving one market. The demand for both networks is the same. Assume the minimum vendor order quantity is 100 units and the demand from each market is a constant five per day. Since no safety stock is required, in the single-warehouse case, inventory will vary from 10 days of supply to zero as inventory is depleted from the minimum order quantity, with an average of five days. In the two-warehouse case, inventory at each warehouse will vary from 20 days to zero, with an average of 10 days in each warehouse. So the single warehouse holds, on average, half the inventory of the combined two warehouses.

Risk pooling effects arise when considering the quantity of safety stock inventory required in a network to meet target service levels. In general, the more centralized a network is, the less safety stock is required to meet a target service level, all else being equal. If we consider the same example as above of one versus two distribution centers serving two different markets, the quantity of safety stock required in the single warehouse case is always less than or equal to the combined quantity in the two warehouse case. How much less depends on how correlated demand is in the two markets. If demand in the two markets is independent (a typical but probably not entirely realistic assumption), the required safety stock to achieve the same service level is about 40% less in the single warehouse case. So the benefits of risk pooling can be significant and should not be ignored in a network rationalization model.

As we discussed how to incorporate inventory holding costs into our model, we concluded that the effect of minimum order quantities on inventory was unlikely to differ significantly from one network configuration to another because the volumes through their existing networks were such that minimum order quantities were not a major driver of inventory. And since we were almost certainly going to recommend a consolidation of warehouse sites, the minimum order quantity restrictions would be even less of an issue in that case. On the other hand, we concluded that the safety stock component of inventory would change materially as the network footprint changed. To incorporate this into the model, we assumed that each network configuration would need to provide a specified in-stock rate for all products at each warehouse location. This would drive a certain safety stock requirement at each warehouse depending on the volume of product handled by the warehouse. To make this manageable, we decided to approximate the inventory costs as a piecewise linear increasing concave function of the flow of products through a warehouse. This is not a perfect representation of inventory costs as a function of volume but it is much better than assuming a purely linear function. To obtain the estimated inventory costs as a function of volume, we utilized historical inventory data from existing warehouses and fit this to a piecewise linear function, as shown in Figure 4.1.

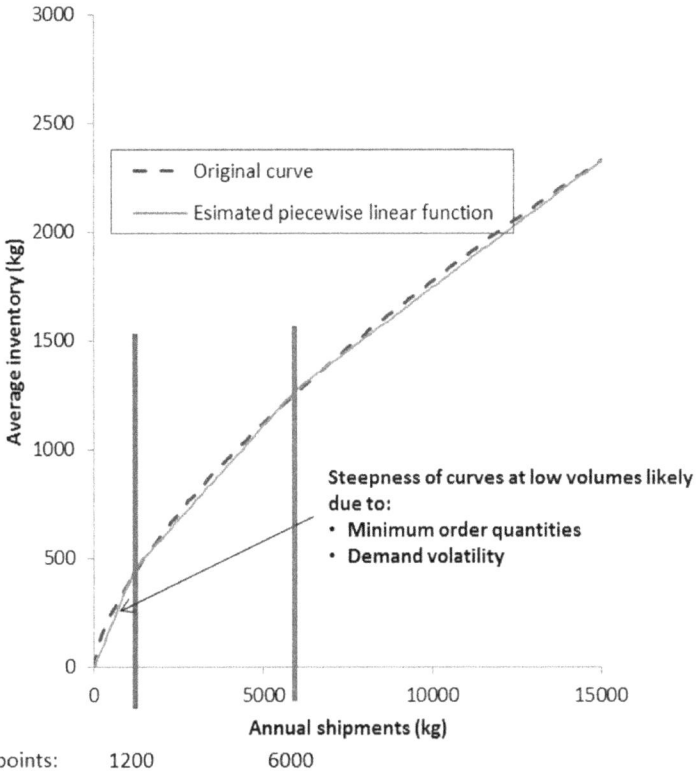

*Figure 4.1  Piecewise linear fit of average inventory as function of annual shipments*

## 4.4    Model Solution

The problem our client was asking us to solve was to find the minimum cost distribution network that would satisfy projected demand, selecting among approximately 20,000 candidate warehouse locations. In evaluating a network configuration, we were looking primarily at annual operating costs, including inventory holding costs (assuming a target in-stock rate), but also at the time required to serve each customer from its closest warehouse.

Because of our modeling simplifications, in particular, the assumption of a piecewise linear inventory cost function and the assumption of linear transportation and variable warehouse operating costs, this problem can be formulated as a non-linear mixed integer optimization problem.

Unfortunately, the number of 0–1 variables in the problem formulation together with the constraints made finding an optimal solution utilizing commercial optimization software impossible. We tried numerous approaches but to no avail; the optimization software consistently failed to find a solution even when left to run for multiple days. We tried to simplify the problem in a variety of ways to reduce the number of integer variables. For example, we decided to reduce the number of candidate warehouse locations by looking at 3-digit zip codes. This reduced the number of possible locations to something under 900. Still, the software could find no solution.

I had been down this path before and knew that this was a likely outcome. The reality is that even with today's powerful optimization software and computer hardware, it is easy to formulate a mixed integer linear optimization problem that is impossible for modern supercomputers to solve within a couple of days. And these are not theoretical problems but real ones that arise in a variety of different business contexts. Fortunately, we had done some contingency planning and had come up with heuristics to find a good but not necessarily optimal solution to the problem. This was our fallback plan and in the end, was the approach we ended up relying on.

The heuristic we designed started with an initial distribution center (DC) selection procedure which worked roughly as follows:

1. Assign each demand (product-destination pair) to DC that can supply it at the lowest cost.
2. For each DC, find the nearest neighbor DC: the DC which is the next least expensive DC from which to satisfy its demand.
3. Find candidate DC to shut down:
   a. For each DC that is open, calculate the net decrease in cost (inventory holding cost reduction plus fixed DC cost reduction minus increased transportation cost plus change in variable DC cost) of moving all demand from the DC to its nearest neighbor.
   b. For the DC with the largest net decrease in cost calculated in step 3a. move all its demand to its nearest neighbor and turn off this DC.
4. Repeat steps 2 and 3: Update nearest neighbor map excluding the DC that was just deleted and calculate next best DC to shut down.

The algorithm stops when no net decrease in cost is possible. This is a straightforward myopic search heuristic. It is worth pointing out that even though the heuristic finds a set of DCs whose costs cannot be reduced by shutting any additional DCs, it may be possible to shift products around within that network to get a net decrease in costs by trading off increased transportation costs against decreased inventory holding costs. We implemented additional procedures to identify if any such opportunities existed. We also implemented a number of other optional modifications to the algorithm, including one which allowed users to specify the fraction of overall demand that could be satisfied within a specified number of days from the nearest warehouse, and one which allowed users to specify a maximum number of warehouses. The heuristics took minutes to run, which allowed us to look at many alternative scenarios.

## 4.5   Model Results and Recommendations

Our model results showed first that the least cost network configuration consisted of 32 warehouse locations, compared with about 100 in the existing network, which was the baseline for our analysis. The resulting estimated annual cost reduction over the baseline scenario was approximately 40 percent with the same fraction of demand that could be satisfied within one day from the closest warehouse. When we restricted selection of warehouse locations only to existing locations, we found that the resulting minimum cost solution was within 2 percent of the greenfield solution. This was an important finding, because it showed that the company could achieve nearly the same cost reduction by sticking with existing warehouse locations, which would be far more feasible and less costly than opening new locations and closing existing locations.

Sensitivity analysis showed that the optimal number of warehouses varied from approximately 25 to 35 as we varied the annual fixed costs of operating a warehouse from +25 percent to −25 percent of our nominal fixed cost estimates. We also observed that near the optimum, the cost function was flat, so that getting the exact number of warehouses right did not seem critical. Figure 4.2 shows the annualized costs of operating the network as a function of the number of warehouses. In the range of approximately 30 to 40, the costs are essentially flat.

Chart: Minimum cost Distribution Network Footprints (cost in $M, stacked bars)

| # of Whses | 10 | 20 | 30 | 40 | 50 | 60 | 70 | 80 | 90 | 100 |
|---|---|---|---|---|---|---|---|---|---|---|
| Total | 115.8 | 96.0 | 91.9 | 92.8 | 95.7 | 100.2 | 105.2 | 111.0 | 116.9 | 123.0 |
| Inventory holding | 25.5 | 26.0 | 26.2 | 26.4 | 26.5 | 26.7 | 26.8 | 26.8 | 26.9 | 26.9 |
| Whse expense | 7.1 | 14.2 | 21.3 | 28.4 | 35.6 | 42.7 | 49.8 | 56.9 | 64.0 | 71.1 |
| Transportation | 83.2 | 55.8 | 44.3 | 37.9 | 33.6 | 30.9 | 28.7 | 27.3 | 26.0 | 24.9 |
| % Dmd satisfied in 1 day | 94.1% | 99.2% | 99.9% | 99.9% | 99.9% | 99.9% | 99.9% | 99.9% | 99.9% | 99.9% |

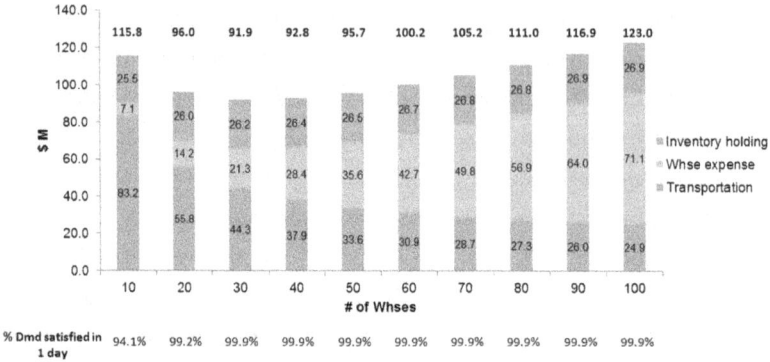

*Figure 4.2  Minimum cost Distribution Network Footprints as Function of Number of Warehouses*

These results were encouraging for the client sponsors because they confirmed what they had suspected all along: that their existing network was far too large and the fixed cost structure of the network was hurting them financially. So while the results were viewed as positive and the recommendation to consolidate their network to approximately one-third the size was accepted, the actual implementation of the recommendations became immediately a much thornier problem. Which warehouses to close? Which warehouses to expand? How to go about doing this in a manner which would not be disruptive to the business and have the least cost impact? No sooner had we finished with our final presentation on our model results than these debates began. The modeling work we had done had pointed the company in the right direction, but the hard work of actually making changes to the business had just begun.

## Endnotes

1. Examples include: Supply Chain Guru sold by Llamasoft, Supply Chain Strategist sold by JDA Software, SAILS sold by Insight Inc., Network Design sold by Infor, OMP Plus sold by OM Partners, Supply Chain Design sold by Quintic.
2. For example, see PC*Miler software.

# CHAPTER 5

# Identifying Inventory and Cycle Time Reduction Opportunities for a Steel Manufacturer

## 5.1 Background

Inventory reduction is a perennial focus in companies looking to cut costs and streamline operations. Cutting inventory is not difficult unless one wants to do it without adversely affecting the company, either by hurting customer service (and thereby decreasing revenue) or by increasing operating costs. A specialty steel manufacturer was looking at ways to reduce inventory at its factories and at the same time, to improve customer service levels. Much of the inventory was in the form of work in process, and looking around the sprawling factory, I could easily understand why management believed that there was excess WIP: ingots of partially processed steel, each weighing many tons and worth many thousands of dollars, lay strewn about on the factory grounds, like an unattractive modern sculpture garden. Many of these ingots had a patina of rust on them, indicating that they had been lying there for some time. With so much WIP, it was plain to see why customer service levels were suffering; the company typically built much of its products to order and too much WIP meant cycle times were high and the ability to meet customer commitments was compromised. But figuring out how to reduce WIP without adversely affecting customer service levels is tricky, as management was well aware of.

The company followed a hybrid *push and pull* manufacturing strategy. End-to-end production lead times for products were long—on the order of several months—and customers typically were not willing to wait that long for products to be produced and delivered. So the company had evolved a process whereby the front-end manufacturing process was mostly *build-to-forecast* and the back-end process was mostly *build-to-order*. In the middle was a strategic buffer where ingots of steel of many different types were held in inventory.

The front-end process started with an electric arc furnace, an expensive asset that the company tried to keep in constant use. The decision of what type of steel to produce in the furnace among the dozens of types to choose from was made by planners who based their decision on aggregate demand forecasts and on scrap metal supply. Whether they made good decisions or not was not something that management could easily judge. Most of the inventory in the strategic buffer was unassigned and therefore available to be utilized to fulfill customer orders. In principle, ingots would be pulled from this strategic buffer when a firm customer order for a specific type and quantity of product came in. In principle, this should work. But many problems can and did arise in practice.

One problem is that it is difficult to maintain the discipline of a pull process in a culture which does not fully embrace it. The concepts of lean manufacturing generally and pull manufacturing in particular were not ingrained in the company. Also, in order for the pull model to work effectively, several things need to be in place. First, the strategic buffer inventory needs to be stocked in such a way that when customer orders arrive, there is enough inventory in the strategic buffer to provide a high off-the-shelf fill rate. Because of the many kinds of steel that the company produced and because demand was volatile, this meant that high levels of inventory were required to be held in the strategic buffer area. But the front-end process was frequently unable to maintain the required inventory in the strategic buffer, either because of insufficient raw material supply or because of production constraints. So, often, firm orders could not be filled from available inventory in the strategic buffer.

Also, even if adequate inventory is held at the strategic buffer supply, when firm orders arrive, if there are too many such orders, then the downstream factory operations will be flooded with work, causing delays and backups. On the other hand, if too few orders materialize, downstream work centers remain idle. Both situations can wreak significant havoc on manufacturing operations. In fact, both situations frequently arose at different times of the year and management dealt with them in precisely the wrong way. In the case of a spike in customer orders, there was no easy way to limit the flow of products into the downstream work centers so these work centers often would get backed up, causing delays. While there had been talk of implementing a kanban system to limit the congestion at work centers, no such system had been deployed. In the case of a lull in customer orders, management was concerned about keeping expensive assets and employees idle and would often resort to filling the available capacity with production orders that were not tied to customer orders, as a way to keep the work centers running. The result was finished goods or partially finished goods that no customers wanted.

This is a typical situation that a company finds itself in. Managers and workers are acutely aware of a problem—in this case, excess inventory and poor customer service levels—but everyone in the company has a different opinion of the root cause and the cure. People talk past each other and there appears to be no way to get consensus on the way forward. Morale suffers and a negative atmosphere pervades the company as problems persist.

Many of the employees whom I had contact with viewed the consulting team which I was part of as troublesome meddlers who were just distracting them from their work. We had been hired precisely to identify the root causes of high inventory and poor customer service and to propose remedies. We had a limited amount of time, just a few months, and there was no shortage of ideas on how to improve system performance. But we lacked a mechanism to test hypotheses on factory improvements before actually implementing them on the shop floor. We needed a way to evaluate proposed fixes that would convince people of the best way to address the problems they were wrestling with. We decided that a simulation model would be the most effective means of testing alternative solutions. With a simulation model of the factory, we could, for example, identify bottleneck work centers, evaluate the impact of implementing a kanban system, and assess the effect of adding or removing shifts from a work center. As it turned out, there was added impetus for us to build a simulation—the C.E.O. of the company, I was told, had specifically asked for a model and so delivering one by the end of the project was a priority.

I knew that undertaking to build a realistic factory simulation in the short time frame that we had was going to be challenging. Constructing the model itself in software would require focused effort and I knew that data collection to populate and validate the model would be difficult. It was a high-risk undertaking, made worse by the fact that the consulting team which I was part of was tasked with a number of other activities. So the building of the simulation would not get the team's undivided attention. Under normal circumstances, I would have pressed to reduce the risk by adding resources, extending our timeline, or cutting back on the scope of the model. But I did not have the leverage in this situation to take any of these actions and was not able to convince those who did that they were necessary.

At first, development of the model went smoothly. We had decided to divide tasks roughly into two separate categories: (1) model design and construction and (2) data collection and processing. I and one other individual would work on designing and coding the simulation while another set of resources, managed separately, would focus on data collection. We made rapid and steady progress in designing and building the simulation. But telltale signs of delays on the data collection side became apparent whenever I inquired about progress. I was told that there were other team priorities, that the data collection effort would not take long, that they had identified the sources for most of the data and so just needed to collect it and get it into the format that the model needed. But no data was forthcoming. Not surprisingly, data collection would prove to be the Achilles heel of the modeling effort.

## 5.2   Designing and Building a Simulation Model

The model of the factory that we undertook to build was a discrete event simulation. This type of simulation works by defining a set of events that can occur in a factory—for example, the completion of processing a job at a work center or the failure of a machine—and then propagating the factory forward in simulated time from event to event, where the underlying assumption is that the state of the factory only changes at the discrete epochs when these events occur. The chief strength of a discrete event simulation is also its greatest challenge; the fact that specific events drive state changes means we only have to keep track of changes to the system at these discrete epochs, which simplifies and speeds up the simulation considerably. At the same time, restricting system changes to event occurrences means you have to be careful about defining the set of events which drive the simulation.

In designing the simulation, we developed an initial list of events that we thought would adequately characterize the factory. They were: the release of a new lot into the factory, the completion of an operation at a work center, the arrival of a lot to a work center, the breakdown of a work center, the repair of a work center, the start of a shift at a work center, and the end of a shift at a work center. Lots, or ingots, would circulate through the factory moving from work center to work center based on their routings.

There were four types of work centers that we chose to model: (1) batch work centers, which could process multiple lots at once up to a specified maximum weight; (2) single lot work centers, which processed one lot at a time, with each lot requiring time proportional to the starting weight of the lot; (3) fixed processing time work centers, which process one lot at a time, with each lot requiring a fixed time regardless of weight; and (4) fixed delay work centers, which cause lots to be delayed for a fixed amount of time. These four types of work centers allowed us to model a variety of different kinds of work centers and activities in the factory.

Discussions about how certain types of activities in the factory would be modeled and how detailed the simulation needed to be occurred frequently both in the design and development phases. A typical example was how to model transportation of a lot from one location in the factory to another, as it progressed through different operations on its way from raw material to finished good. The process as we observed it typically started with a transport worker getting notified to move an ingot from one location to another. He obtains a vehicle appropriate to transport the lot. He proceeds to drive the vehicle to the location where the lot is located. He locates the lot and loads it onto the vehicle. He drives to the desired drop-off location. He arrives at the drop-off location and unloads the lot. He completes documentation to indicate that the move is complete.

We needed to decide the appropriate level of detail at which to model this transport process. Fundamentally, we had to ask ourselves whether we believed that the transport of lots between operations was a significant driver of inventory in the factory. Did it cause or contribute significantly to bottlenecks? If the answer was no, we would want to model the transport process in a relatively high-level way or not at all. If the answer was yes, we would model the process in greater detail. Some people might argue that there is no way to categorically answer this question without actually testing the hypothesis within the model. If unchecked, this reasoning leads to always erring on the side of more detail, not less, and to models that thereby become hopelessly complex.

In this case, we concluded that while transport did contribute meaningfully to cycle time of lots because transport times were often significant, we did not believe that transport operations were a source of bottlenecks or congestion in the factory. So, we decided to include transport operations in our model to capture their impact on overall cycle times but not go so far as to model the resources (a transport worker and a vehicle) necessary to transport a lot. From a modeling perspective, then, a transport operation would be modeled as a visit to a fixed delay work center where the delay would be specified as a probability distribution. For example, let us say that the time to move a lot between two work centers typically takes between 15 and 20 minutes. We would model this transport process as visiting a fixed delay work center with a processing time that is uniformly distributed between 15 and 20 minutes. If we were fortunate enough to have a historical record of sample transport times, we could fit those samples to a distribution and use this distribution in our model. More likely, these would be rough estimates obtained from either direct observation or from conversations with workers.

It is worth emphasizing how our choice of modeling transport operations directly affects the data collection effort (and vice versa). By including the transport operations in our model, we put an onus on the data collection team to collect and analyze data about transport times. On the other hand, our decision to model transport operations in the way that we did allowed for the possibility of ignoring transport altogether: If a user wanted to, he could either leave out the transport operations in the input data altogether or could specify the distribution as a constant value taking zero time. So, ultimately, our modeling choice in this case gave the model users an option, but not the obligation, to include transport times in the model.

It is also worth pointing out that as model builders, we could easily construct a much more detailed model of transport to reflect what in fact happens in the factory. This would require a great deal more input data. But to what end? We must decide if the effort to build a more detailed model of lot transportation is going to add substantial value to our model. If we were specifically interested in studying the transport of lots within the factory, perhaps such detail would be warranted. Or if we had a working hypothesis that transport was one of the major bottlenecks in the factory, then maybe such detail would be justified. But in the absence of these concerns, there is no reason to introduce additional complexity into the model.

One might object—how can you know a priori that the transport of lots is not of central concern? Isn't it true that we don't know what the cause of the WIP build-up is and couldn't transport be one of the root causes? This is a valid objection. On the other hand, our model of transport can at least be utilized to see the impact that transport time has on system performance. In keeping with the principle of model parsimony, we felt that keeping the model of transport simple at first was justifiable. If our modeling results led us to conclude that a more nuanced model of transport was required, we could always add that in a subsequent version of the model.

We had similar discussions about a range of factory operations. These included whether to explicitly model workers in the factory as resources necessary to perform operations (we decided not to), whether to allow multiple parallel machines at a work center or whether to model each work center as single machine (we decided on the latter), and whether to explicitly model work shifts or to assume a certain amount of up time for each work center (we decided on the former). Each time, we had to think through carefully the ramifications of each of our choices.

## 5.3    Considerations in Constructing a Discrete Event Simulation

In building the discrete event simulation, as with any model, we had the choice of using a special purpose simulation software package, of which there are many to choose from,[1] or building one from scratch using a general purpose programming language. This is a variant of the usual make or buy decision. The commercial simulation software packages have the advantage that they don't require users to have programming skills; one can construct simulations using a graphical user interface. This sounds appealing but is really only valuable when constructing simple models for pedagogical purposes. Building a large scale model by dragging and dropping icons on a palate quickly becomes frustrating and inefficient. The other major advantage of using commercial simulation packages is the rich set of animation features that the packages provide. If you are building a simulation to show people what a system will physically look like when operating, these packages provide a quick and relatively easy way to accomplish this. Building a detailed computer animation in a general purpose programming language would require far greater effort. In fact, most of what you are paying for when you buy a commercial simulation package is the ability to create animated simulations quickly and easily. That is where the vast majority of software development effort in these packages is spent. If this capability is not a high priority—and in our situation, it was not—the advantages of using a commercial package can quickly be outweighed by their disadvantages.

I have used commercial simulation languages extensively and have identified a long list of disadvantages that apply to many of them:

- **Run-time performance issues.** For a variety of reasons, run-time performance of models developed in commercial simulation packages is generally poorer than models developed in general purpose languages. Even with animation turned off, run-time performance is still quite poor. For example, I have done benchmark comparisons between simulations built in Arena and in C for the same system and have observed a factor of approximately 10 speed up when using C. This is an important consideration when you anticipate running a large number of simulations and face time constraints.

- **Language deficiencies.** Some of the proprietary simulation languages lack basic features of modern procedural and functional programming languages, such as the ability to define objects, encapsulation, etc. For example, SIMAN which is the language underlying simulation software package Arena, has no object-oriented nor functional programming features. As such, it is extremely difficult to write complex simulation code in SIMAN that is easy to follow and maintain.

- **Development licensing restrictions.** Many of the packages have complex licensing structures that allow users full access to the capabilities of the software only if they purchase the most expensive licenses. The cost of a single seat unrestricted development license for some of these packages can be quite expensive while the cost of general purpose language compilers and integrated development environments are often free.

- **Run-time licensing restrictions.** Most of the packages do not allow users to create stand-alone applications that can run without a run-time license, unlike all general purpose programming languages. If you are developing a simulation for a client, this means that any client who wishes to run the simulation you develop will have to acquire a run-time license. This can become a major barrier to acceptance.

- **Difficult data input mechanisms.** If you build a simulation using a graphical user interface, the effort required to populate data for the model can be significant as the size of the simulation grows. Take, for example, the workflow for defining a piece of machinery in a factory simulation. You would typical drag and drop an object representing a generic piece of machinery from an object menu to the modeling workspace. Then you need to double click on the object and navigate to the appropriate screens to enter processing times, failure and repair times and distributions, resource requirements, etc. If you are doing this for a simple model consisting of a few pieces of machinery, this workflow may be acceptable. But if you were to construct, for example, a simulation of a realistic sized semiconductor fab using this

approach, you would need to repeat this manual process
several hundred times to represent all of the workstations
in the factory. Also, the ability to quickly find and modify a
piece of data for one particular workstation becomes difficult
as the number of workstations increases. Clearly, the approach
does not scale well to large and complex models. What is
lacking in these packages is the ability to create a simulation
in which the user only needs to populate data tables in order
to define the entire system that is to be simulated.

- **Awkward custom user interfaces.** The development
  environments in these packages typically allow developers
  to create custom user interfaces, but the environments are
  typically proprietary and require a steep learning curve to get
  to the point where a developer can easily construct a custom
  interface.

- **Complex and inflexible interfaces with external databases
  and Excel.** The ability to link to external databases and Excel
  in order to populate models or report results is generally
  supported by many of these packages but these interfaces are
  often not so easy to exploit nor do they have the flexibility
  that developers typically want.

- **Difficulty separating model logic from data.** By model
  logic, I mean the description of the flow of entities through
  a network of resources, where entities can represent
  physical or logical phenomena. By model data, I mean the
  specifications necessary to instantiate a logical model so that
  it can be simulated. So, for example, the model logic for
  a factory simulation would consist of a description of the
  flow of physical products through the factory, the sequence
  of operations that each product undergoes at which work
  centers, the logic of how resource contention is resolved
  (e.g. scheduling discipline at a particular work center) and
  how flow control is achieved (e.g. a Kanban mechanism).
  The model data in this case would specify the processing
  time distributions for each of the operations at work centers,
  the quantity of available resources at each work center,

the Kanban sizes, the probabilities of rework or yield, etc. Separating model logic from model data is good practice as it makes it easier to determine if the logic is correct without worrying about specific data, and it makes running multiple scenarios easy because the data can be modified without touching the model logic. Most graphical user interface (GUI) simulation environments blur the distinction between model logic and model data.

• **Access to a relatively small user community.** Most simulation packages have small user bases relative to the user base for general purpose programming languages. It is therefore harder to seek out help in user forums and other online communities.

If you are using a general purpose programming language to construct a simulation, you can make use of discrete event simulation libraries that have been written in these languages or which have application programming interfaces (APIs) available in these languages. Many of these are open source and are free to use. On the other hand, object libraries are of variable quality, often have steep learning curves and may not have extensive and well-written documentation so leveraging these libraries carries its own set of risks.

## 5.4   Core Components of a Discrete Event Simulation

We decided fairly early on to construct the discrete event simulation using a general purpose programming language. To the uninitiated, creating a discrete event simulation from scratch in a general purpose programming language may seem daunting but is in fact quite straightforward. It also carries with it the distinct advantage that once you have written the underlying core components of a simulation, reusing these components for other simulation projects becomes quite simple.

These core components are well known and have been written about extensively in books and articles on the subject of discrete event simulation.[2] In constructing our simulation, we leveraged both existing code from previous simulation projects as well as open source code. We also wrote code from scratch where necessary. Below is a summary of the core components of any discrete event simulation, together with observations from my experiences building this and other discrete event simulations:

**A pseudo-random number generator (PRNG):** Much has been written on the subject of PRNGs. Suffice it to say that it is worth using one that has been thoroughly tested. Do not try to write your own. There is plenty of open source code available that implement high-quality, long-period PRNGs, including the Mersenne Twister, which has a practically infinite period. Linear congruential generators have lost some of their luster with the demonstration that they fail certain tests of randomness but they are still valid for use in many circumstances. Generally, PRNGs return an independent sample from a uniform [0,1] distribution on each call. Whatever code you use, you want to make sure that you can draw multiple sample streams from the PRNG where each sample stream is initiated with an input seed and where the streams are guaranteed to be far enough apart that they will not overlap in any reasonable length simulation.

**Random variate generators:** These are routines that utilize the PRNG to generate samples from desired distributions. Routines for generating samples for a wide variety of distributions using a PRNG as input are widely available in many languages. Do not bother writing your own code unless you are so inclined. Many general purpose languages have built-in random variate generators. Don't use these unless you can control the PRNG stream to utilize on a given call to the routine.

**An event priority queue:** This is the core of a discrete event simulation: a list of all the currently scheduled future events, sorted in increasing order in which they occur. Most of the books on discrete event simulation do not go into detail on how to implement an event priority queue. Events may be large objects, so it is not recommended that events themselves be placed into the priority queue, but rather pointers to the events. You can use standard priority queue implementations available in most object-oriented languages like Java and C++ (although Java does not easily support the use of pointers). A good way to implement an event priority queue is to store pointers to events in the priority queue, sorted based on the time at which the events occur.[3] Information about the events themselves are stored in the event structure. Pointers to unused events are stored in a stack. When a new event needs to be scheduled, you pop an event off the event stack, specify the time it's going to occur, and place a pointer to the event into the priority queue. When you've finished processing an event, push it back on the stack so it can be reused. Generally speaking, you will need some special purpose functions to manipulate the event priority queue and these may not be available in the standard implementation for priority queues. For example, you may need to search through the priority queue to find a specific future event so that it can be rescheduled. This requires removing the event from the queue, changing its occurrence time and re-inserting it into the priority queue.

**An event management loop:** This is the central loop in a discrete event simulation. It is usually quite short, consisting of at most a dozen or so lines of code. The loop consists of removing the next event from the event priority queue, advancing the simulation time to the time of this event, then calling the appropriate routine to handle the processing of this type of event.

**An entity stack:** A reusable collection of entities, which represent the physical or logical items flowing through the system being modeled. Entities can have many types and the object that defines an entity may have a lot of attributes. Therefore, just as with the event priority queue, it is preferable to manipulate pointers to entities, rather than entities themselves. The stack would consist then not of entities themselves, but pointers to entities. When an entity is needed, a pointer is popped off the stack and utilized as appropriate. When it exits the system and is no longer needed, it is pushed back onto the stack for reuse.

**Statistics collection logic:** The point of the simulation is to measure system performance. The purpose of statistics collection logic is to update all of the measurements of interest at each event occurrence. Care should be taken to update statistics only for those measurements that have changed at the event occurrence. A naïve approach will update all measurements at each event occurrence regardless of whether the event causes a change in the value of a measurement. This will work, but will lead to highly inefficient simulation code. It is worth taking the time to write code that only updates a measurement when an event causes its value to change. It can lead to significant run-time speed improvements especially in complex simulations.

**Event logic:** This is the code that describes how the model handles each type of event when it occurs. As the simulation proceeds, events are processed one by one by the event management loop. Inside the loop, a call is made to the appropriate event logic routine to handle that type of event. This logic will likely change whenever a new simulation model is created so it is important to keep the event logic separate from other parts of the simulation code.

Creating all of these components for the first time requires some effort. But once the components have been created, reusing them to construct new simulations is quite simple. Anyone with reasonable skills in a general purpose programming language should be able to construct a discrete event simulation from scratch without great difficulty. It is enjoyable, results in highly efficient and portable simulation code, and provides great flexibility to the simulation developer because the code can be re-used in many different configurations.

## 5.5   A Critical Failure

The model that we developed had a simple user interface within Excel. It was completely data-driven in that to run a scenario, a user only needed to populate a set of input data tables specified in worksheets within Excel. The data required to run a scenario included:

- A list of all the work centers in the factory along with the number of shifts each work center was in operation each week and their failure and repair time distributions. For batch work centers, the maximum batch size and a

specification of which lots processed at the work center could
be batched together.
- A list of all the products produced in the factory, along with
the production start schedule for each product.
- The routings for each product which specified the sequence
of operations performed on each product together with the
work center at which each operation is performed and the
processing time distribution of each operation.

All of this data existed in some form within the information systems
maintained by the company. We knew that obtaining it, analyzing it, and
processing it into a form in which we could use it, would take significant
effort.

We completed the testing of the model within about one month of
the end of the project. If the data collection effort had been largely complete by then, we would have had just enough time in the remaining one
month to validate the model and run experiments.

Unfortunately, the data collection effort had stalled because the
manager responsible for data collection had deprioritized it in favor
of other activities. His reasoning was that because the simulation was
not yet complete, he could push off data collection without putting
the timeline at risk. He vastly underestimated the time required to collect and analyze the data for the simulation. Ultimately, we ran out of
time before the model data could be adequately scrubbed. As a result, a
validated data set was never fully completed and the model could never
really be put to use. While we left the simulation with the client and
provided training and documentation on its use, we knew that without
a validated data set, the model would not likely be utilized.

Failures are never easy to acknowledge or discuss but I think it is both
honest and necessary to recognize that many modeling efforts do not succeed. The reasons for failure are varied but understanding them is the first
step in not repeating them. Many people involved in this project might
not admit that the simulation modeling effort failed. They might say that
we built and delivered the model as we had promised. But the model
never really got utilized. In this case, the failure had nothing to do with
the model itself. The problem was, as it often is, with the data collection

effort. But in the end, a model that is not utilized cannot be viewed as successful regardless of the cause.

## Endnotes

1. Examples of simulation software solutions include: Promodel, Arena, FlexSim, AutoMod, ExtendSim, and AnyLogic.
2. See, for example, Law and Kelton (1991), Banks, Carson, and Nelson (1996), and Bratley, Fox, and Schrage (1987).
3. When I refer to the use of pointers, I am assuming that you are utilizing a language that enables the use of pointers. If you are using a language like Java, which does not easily support the use of pointers, you may end up sacrificing some run-time performance in your simulation by not being able to use pointers explicitly.

# CHAPTER 6

# Optimizing Inventory Distribution for a Musical Instrument Rental Company

I have found a consistent pattern that arises in most consulting engagements. At the start of the project, spirits are high and people are energized. The executive who is sponsoring the work gives a rousing introduction to the business and provides his perspective on the problem we are tasked with addressing. We meet with various stakeholders and rapidly climb the learning curve of understanding the company's business and its challenges. Usually, by the end of the first few days, we feel like we have a pretty good sense of what the problem is and how we are going to go about tackling it. We think we have a clear path forward, that the case is cracked.

I refer to this point as the peak of ignorance. It is followed by a rapid descent into the valley of despair as we come to realize that all of our initial optimism is based on a naïve and superficial understanding of the company's business and that the actual challenges are far more complex and intractable than we originally believed. This is when the real work starts. Slowly, over weeks, we emerge from the valley of despair as we start to appreciate the nuances of the business and formulate a new way forward.

Business problems, especially ones that consultants are brought in to solve, are never easy. If they were, the consultants would not be needed. When I was starting out in my career, I would sometimes attempt to describe my work to my mother, a practical and smart woman who viewed the corporate world with distrust and was not known for her subtlety. I would describe whatever project I was currently working on and her response would invariably be some form of "Isn't that just common sense? What do they need you for?" I found it hard to argue with her reasoning. But I secretly took some consolation in her harsh response by realizing that I had managed to convince her through my description that what was after all a fairly complex business problem had a pretty straightforward solution. But that was after much hard work studying the problem. She was benefitting, without realizing it, from my distillation of the problem to its basics that had occurred only after months of study.

Often the models I build are really just an application of common sense rules. But incorporating them into a tool that clients can use to make decisions is not always obvious. A good example is a decision support tool that we built for a musical instrument rental company. The company's main business is renting band and orchestral instruments to primary and secondary school students. While rentals can occur year round, the bulk of their business occurs at the start of the school year when students typically enroll in bands or orchestra, from August through October. In preparation for this peak rental season, the company forecasts approximately how many instruments of each type it will need in each school district and then decides how many of these instruments can be provided through refurbishment of previously used and returned instruments and how many new instruments need to be purchased. In the months leading up to the start of the peak rental season, the company needs to prepare for the peak rental season by making sure adequate rental instruments are shipped to stores in advance throughout their network, so that when students request instruments, there is high likelihood of the instrument being available for rental from the store. The challenge for the business is figuring out how many instruments to ship out to each store and how to balance the need for providing good customer service while not exceeding the ability of the distribution network to handle the volume of instruments shipped each week.

The company's distribution network consists of a main distribution center where instruments are refurbished and new instruments are received from vendors, a set of regional distribution centers which receive replenishments from the main distribution center, and the retail stores which receive shipments from regional distribution centers. The company prefers to keep inventory centralized as much as possible so as to avoid excess shipping costs; if instruments are shipped to stores or regional warehouses, there is a chance that those instruments will need to be rerouted to other locations if there are inventory imbalances. This leads to situations in which instruments may end up being shipped from the central DC to a regional DC, then to a store, then shipped from the store to another store in a different geographic region, resulting in excess shipping costs that would have been avoided if the inventory were kept centrally.

The company had for many years managed this process in an ad-hoc way: the DC managers would make a call each week on how much inventory to ship out to regional DCs and how much inventory the regional DCs should ship out to rental locations. This process was inefficient and subject to variable results, depending on the capabilities of the different DC managers. We were asked to design a software model that would determine the right quantity of instruments to ship out from the central DC to the regional DCs, and from the regional DCs to the rental stores each week based on the current inventory at each location and the latest rental projections. The idea was to remove reliance on guesswork and intuition of the DC managers and make decisions on inventory transfers in a more systematic and transparent way.

The model would need to have flexibility in trading off the many objectives and constraints we had heard about during our initial discussions. These objectives included:

- Maximizing the quantity of demand satisfied on time
- Maximizing the satisfaction of customer preferences
- Minimizing safety stock deficits at rental locations, regional DCs and central DC
- Minimizing the number of transfers of instruments and making transfers as late as possible
- Minimizing the amount of inventory held downstream in the network
- Maximizing the fairness of distribution of instruments across rental locations

Satisfaction of customer preferences referred to the fact that some band and orchestra directors had preferences for certain instrument brands. The company did not usually guarantee that students would receive their preferred brands when renting instruments but to the extent that it was possible, it was viewed as a plus for customer service if those brand preferences could be satisfied. Safety stock deficits measured the amount by which inventory fell below safety stock targets at stocking locations. This objective related to wanting to maintain inventory above these targets when possible. The safety stock targets were not viewed as hard constraints. The fairness of distribution instruments across rental locations reflected the idea that, all else being equal, it is preferable to allocate instruments and brands equitably across different rental locations in proportion to the quantity of instruments that each location rents. This fairness metric could be implemented as a min-max objective function.

The constraints included:

- Not exceeding the volume of instruments that could be handled (received and/or shipped) at a location per week
- Not exceeding the shipping lane constraints between locations
- Amount shipped during a week from a location cannot exceed the balance on hand at the beginning of the week
- Inventory balance equations at each location must hold: balance on hand at end of week = balance on hand from prior week + quantity that flows in during the week - the quantity allocated out

The way we envisioned that the model would be utilized is that each week, up-to-date information about inventory and rental projections would be fed to the model. Using this information, the model would generate a plan for shipping instruments that attempted to meet the objectives specified by management while respecting constraints on shipment volumes and inventory availability. The plan would provide a week-by-week statement of how many instruments of each type to ship from location to location. The only portion of the plan that would be executed would be the current week's plan. In subsequent weeks, the model would be re-run with refreshed data to obtain a refreshed shipment plan.

The challenge for us was to come up with a model that would specify the "correct" number of instruments of each type to ship from location to location. We realized quickly that the problem could be formulated as a multi-period linear program where the objective function was maximizing the quantity of demand that could be satisfied at the retail locations from available inventory. The constraints would capture the limits on volumes that could be handled by each DC by week, transportation lane limitations between locations, and the inventory balance equations. This was fine as a starting point but we soon realized that the solution to this linear program was not a single plan but a range of possible plans, because there were many possible ways of meeting the demand for instruments each week while satisfying the constraints. To take a simple example, if the demand for an instrument in Week 10 is 100 at a rental location, and we have 100 instruments available at the start of Week 1 at the central DC, there are many ways of satisfying that demand: we can ship 100 instruments in Week 1 to the rental location, or 100 instruments in Week 2, etc.; or 50 in Week 1, 50 in Week 2, etc. All of these solutions will be feasible and optimal solutions.

This suggested a modification to our solution approach that would incorporate concepts from goal programming. Rather than solving a single linear program, our model would solve a series of nested linear programs, where the optimal solution to the previous linear program would be incorporated as a constraint in the subsequent linear program. This allowed us to formulate a model in which management could change the results of the model based on the priority they gave to different objectives. It would provide the needed flexibility that managers wanted to manipulate the instrument allocation plan based on trading off these different objectives.

The solution we implemented did precisely this. There were six nested linear programs, each with an objective function corresponding to one of the objectives listed above. The model we delivered was greeted with enthusiasm but we knew that adoption would only come after much struggle. One of the problems that immediately arose was that the DC managers complained that the transfer orders generated by the model couldn't be executed because of insufficient balance on hand. In other words, the solution that the model generated often specified shipment of instruments that exceeded what was available at a location. The problem was traced back to the fact that data that the model received from the company's transaction systems that specified the shipments received by a DC during a week sometimes reflected what was shipped to a location during a week but not necessarily what was actually received by the DC by the shipment cutoff date. The issue arose because the model viewed the world in weekly increments and assumed that any shipments due to arrive to a location in a given week would be available for shipment out of that location that week. In reality, some shipments arrived late in the week, well after the shipment cutoff date for the week. Problems of this sort—where there is a mismatch in the data that the model receives and what is actually true on the ground—happen all the time. In many situations, the mismatch does not create any serious problem but in this case, it led to transfer orders that the DC managers could not execute. If the problem is not fixed right away, the people using the tool can quickly lose faith in it. In this situation, the remedy was fairly simple: limit the available inventory in a given week to what was available on hand at the start of the week plus what was due to arrive to the location prior to the shipment cutoff date.

Another problem was the run-time performance of the model. The model was originally designed to calculate a weekly allocation plan over a 52-week horizon. The resulting goal program took several days to solve on the client's server, which had ample memory and computational power. The client complained that the solution time was too long. They would kick off the model to run at the start of the weekend but it would not find a solution by the end of the weekend. In order to be workable, the solution needed to be available first thing Monday morning. We were puzzled about why the solution of a series of linear programs, whose size was large but should have been solvable within hours or minutes, would take so long. We investigated and discovered that the problem was not with the solution of the linear program perse, which took only minutes to solve, but the pre-processing of the problem. To implement the goal program, we used OPL, a modeling language developed by IBM. OPL, like other modeling languages for linear and mixed integer programming, is intended to provide a platform to easily specify the objective and constraints of a linear program.

We had worked extensively with AMPL before, a competitor of OPL, and were inclined to use it for this project. But IBM made OPL available for free with the licensing of CPLEX, which was the linear programming solver that we were using. So to save the client some money, we decided to use OPL.

When we examined where the computational effort was being spent, it turned out that most of the effort—at least 90 percent of the CPU time—was by OPL translating the model into CPLEX readable form. This was puzzling to us and we strongly suspected that OPL had some significant defects in its code that slowed its performance unreasonably. Some preliminary tests indicated that the performance of OPL was significantly inferior to AMPL.[1] However, we were unable to get IBM to even acknowledge that it was an issue, let alone to address the issue in a timely fashion. Instead, we took actions to simplify our problem formulation to improve run-time performance. These actions were not straightforward and required some significant changes to our problem formulation but ultimately, through a series of modifications, we were able to find an approach that could solve within a time period that was acceptable to the client.

I mention these issues to illustrate some of the practical challenges that we faced in implementing what seemed initially like a fairly straightforward model. One of the lessons learned is that when relying on a third party software solution for developing a model, make sure that you have thoroughly tested the software and confirmed that it will work acceptably at scale. We made the mistake of accepting IBM's assurances that OPL would perform just as well as other modeling languages but did not perform any testing to confirm their assertions.

We also did not make enough of an investment in time to sit in person with the model users once the model was up and running to address issues as they arose. There is a difference between being available on the phone or via email to respond to questions, versus being present in person at the client site to address issues as they arise. This may seem like a small distinction but can make a big difference especially when a model is first being put through its paces. By not being present, we were increasing the risk that small problems could metastasize into negative perceptions about the model, eventually leading people to stop relying on the model.

## Endnotes

1. I make no claims about OPL's performance today, only what I observed at the time that this work was conducted. It is conceivable that progress has been made in addressing OPL's run-time performance over the last few years.

# CHAPTER 7

# Modeling for Modeling's Sake

## A Cautionary Tale

Computer models are only useful if they provide a solution to a problem. This sounds obvious but software developers can sometimes lose sight of this basic fact. I worked for about three years at i2 Technologies, a supply chain software company that has since been acquired by JDA software. I was a solution architect for one of their flagship products that had recently been released called Supply Chain Planner (SCP). SCP was championed as a revolutionary software solution that would enable companies to vastly improve their supply chain performance through improved planning. How the software would do this was somewhat mysterious, but never mind, this was at a time when the hype around supply chain software was reaching a fever pitch. Companies in manufacturing, distribution, and retail businesses were rushing to spend millions of dollars on supply chain software. The promise was that by improving the way companies planned and executed the purchase of supplies, the manufacture of products, and the shipment and storage of goods, companies could save millions of dollars in inventory and operating expenses while at the same time improving customer service levels.

Certainly, it was easy to recognize, as it still is today, that there are vast inefficiencies in the way that supply chains operate. But making improvements to address these inefficiencies, as anyone knows who has tried, is usually not straightforward. Companies looking for a silver bullet found supply chain software companies eager to sell them software which promised to transform their supply chains without great sacrifice—just writing a check for the software and its implementation.

Being a solution architect meant that I was responsible for designing a specific solution for a customer once the software was purchased. A naïve person might ask why this was necessary. After all, if the software is all that it is cracked up to be, shouldn't the customer just be able to populate the software input tables with the appropriate data and let the software do the rest? It turns out that SCP was much more of a general purpose supply chain modeling environment than it was an off-the-shelf software solution. In order to create a workable solution for a client, you needed to use the proprietary language of SCP to define a supply chain model for the client. Once the model was defined, one could populate the model with data. Then, in principle, the instantiated model could be used for planning. But I discovered as I became more familiar with the product, that there was a big missing link in the software that made utilizing it for planning purposes of limited value: There was no built-in capability in the software to perform any automated planning, which was the entire reason for the software's being. It turned out that to automate planning within SCP, you had to write your own code using SCP's proprietary programming language (which I will gratuitously add, was an abomination, but that is for another discussion).

What do I mean by automated planning? The most challenging types of problems that production planners typically wrestle with are those in which there are constraints of various types present. On the supply side, there may be constraints on availability of parts or on resources that prevent building the entire volume of products that are needed in the required time frame. On the demand side, there may be different priorities given to different products or orders based on customer requirements or the perceived importance of different customers. The general question that planning processes are trying to address in this context is: Given the constraints on resources and material supply, what products should be built and in what sequence, in order to optimize some objective function. The objective function might be to minimize the total lateness of orders, or it might be to maximize profit (assuming all products that are produced can be sold at specified prices), or it might be to maximize the number of customer orders, weighted by priority, that can be fulfilled in a given time frame. The range of possible objectives is large. In reality, every company has a different set of objectives that it is focused on and these objectives are usually competing. So companies typically want to understand the trade-offs between these objectives. A good automated planning system is one which allows the planners to quickly look at plans based on different objectives, and allow them to make trade-offs among them to arrive at a final plan.

To illustrate using a simple example, suppose you are in charge of a factory that produces two products. The factory has five work centers and to produce each product requires processing time on each work center. Each product has a selling price and a raw material cost. You are told that there is maximum amount of production per month for each product that should not be exceeded. There is a fixed cost for operating the factory per month and there are a fixed number of hours per month that each work center is available for production. The planning problem in this context is this: how much of each product to produce in order to maximize profit without violating production constraints—specifically, not exceeding the time available at each work center and not producing more than the maximum quantity of each product. The problem is not difficult to solve using a computer. The problem can be formulated as a linear program and solved using standard linear programming software. The solution to this problem by a computer is a simple example of automated planning. In the much more complex setting of a real factory, the constraints may be much more complex and there may be multiple, conflicting planning objectives but the basic planning problem is much the same: how to arrive at a plan to produce products that achieves certain stated objectives while not violating material and resource constraints.

Another simple example that was widely discussed at i2 was the veggie pizza problem. This was the problem of allocating pizza slices among a group of diners, some of whom are vegetarians, who will only eat pizzas with non-meat toppings. Non-vegetarians will eat pizzas both with and without meat toppings. If I order a selection of meat and non-meat pizzas and allow people to take slices in random order, it is likely that some vegetarians will end up with fewer slices than they would like, but there will be meat slices left over that no one has eaten—clearly, a less-than-optimal outcome. Of course, if we let the vegetarians take their slices first, this situation will not arise. But as a general problem, it illustrates the challenge of allocating a scarce resource (veggie pizzas) among a heterogeneous population of users or consumers of that resource to achieve some stated objective. This, in a greatly simplified form, is an example of a constrained production planning problem.

It was these kinds of planning problems that an automated planning solution like SCP was supposed to be able to solve. But if you purchased the software with the expectation that it would have embedded in it the algorithms necessary to solve these planning problems, you were in for a rude awakening. There were no built-in capabilities to solve these problems, only a modeling environment which allowed you to build a representative model of your supply chain and a language to write an algorithm to solve the planning problem. It was as if you had thought you had purchased a house but found that what you really had purchased were some building materials and some poor quality tools.

My first experience as solution architect was with a disk drive manufacturer who had purchased SCP along with a suite of other products from i2. I was new to the company and had just received training on SCP prior to starting this project. The training left me only with a rudimentary understanding of SCP. It was a complex product and no one seemed quite sure how to use it. My job was to work with the client to figure out how to model their supply chain within SCP so as to enable them to use it for planning purposes. The object model for SCP was enormously complex; it was designed to be able to model just about any kind of manufacturing, distribution, retail, or service operation in exquisite detail. As a result, there were a huge number of objects to choose from in constructing a model for a client. How to choose? There were virtually no guidelines given to me. So I proceeded to pick and choose those objects that seemed to me to be most appropriate for the task at hand and assembled them into what, for me, looked like a reasonable representation of the client's supply chain.

There was another i2 employee working with me on the project who had been involved in other SCP projects. He described to me the phenomenon which he called modeling ecstasy, which was the act of creating a hyper-detailed representation of a supply chain simply for the pleasure of being able to model it, not because there was anything you could actually do with it. Because of the huge number of objects available in SCP, one could create arbitrarily complex and detailed models of supply chains, down to the finest level of granularity. For example, you could model each and every machine in a factory if you wanted to and every last screw in a complex product. And because this capability existed, people assumed that it was perfectly OK, in fact desirable, to represent things at such excruciating levels of detail.

But what could one do with the model once you created it? It turned out—not much. One could create fabulously complex models within SCP of virtually any supply chain but the resulting model was of no value for planning purposes because the software had no built-in capability to automatically construct a feasible plan once a model was specified. It was up to the implementer to write code in the proprietary language of SCP to solve the planning problem. And, of course, very few were up to this task.

The only solvers that were built-in to SCP, according to what we were told, were so-called local solvers. In the generic documentation for the software, these local solvers, based on simulated annealing, would automatically generate plans once your supply chain model had been specified. But these turned out to be hollow claims. All that these appeared to be able to do was to automatically rearrange some plans that were infeasible to make them feasible in a very narrow way. So for example, if there were plans calling for the production of widgets on a particular resource and the production plans violated capacity constraints of the resource, the local solvers could be invoked to automatically reschedule the production plans so that the capacity constraint would no longer be violated. But the resulting plan might then violate a constraint on an upstream or downstream resource. Such was the nature of a local solver. The local solvers had no ability to solve for a plan in a globally optimal way, or even to find a plan that was globally feasible, meaning that it did not violate resource or material constraints.

One of the fundamental problems with SCP was that there was no way to specify an overall objective for a plan such as maximizing profit or minimizing total lateness of orders. As such, it lacked a basic capability that planners required. Some at i2 claimed that this shortcoming of SCP was by design; the fact that there were no built-in solvers provided to solve the underlying planning problems was a feature, not a bug. But this was just nonsense. This was truly a case of a software solution with a rich set of modeling features but lacking any useful function.

Many people at i2, not among the software developers, but among those who, like me, were tasked with actually implementing something useful for our clients, developed ad-hoc algorithms with limited success. In one case, we exported the data from SCP to a linear programming model that was developed separately from SCP which was then solved by Cplex and its solution forced back into SCP. Not an elegant solution but it shows the extent to which implementers were forced to go in order to provide a workable solution to clients. In another case, some heuristics were coded within the language of SCP that attempted to find plans that optimized stated objectives. But these heuristics generally worked poorly. In the end, many implementations of SCP failed because the software was unable to provide the basic planning functionality that planners required. It is hard enough to get planners to adopt a new planning tool when the tool is an obvious improvement over their existing tools. When the tool is not an obvious improvement, adoption will almost certainly fail.

Although I never had the opportunity to talk with the software designers of SCP, I believe, based on my experience and knowledge of the product, that they must have had a grand vision for how SCP was going to be used in an enterprise. SCP would provide a virtual representation of every activity in a supply chain, down to the specific time in seconds when each activity would start and when it would end, exactly what resources it would utilize, what materials it would consume, and what products it would produce. The intention seemed to be that the people who managed the supply chain would keep the virtual representation of all of these activities in sync with the actual supply chain in a way which was never fully articulated. So a user of the software, a planner, could simply make a change in the virtual plan and those plans would somehow be communicated to the real world and be executed there. The designers, I imagine, viewed the software as way to virtually control a supply chain but the mechanism by which this control would be exercised seems never to have been thought through. The software embodied a naïve but ambitious view that a supply chain could be completely manipulated through software. To me, this vision represented a fundamental misreading of what planning software should be, which is, first and foremost, a decision support system for planners. To provide an effective decision support system, one must first start with a deep understanding of what planners in a company are trying to accomplish. The SCP designers did not seem to have any real interest in this. Rather, they started with a preconceived notion of what they thought planners should be doing, which turned out to be rather different from what they actually do.

One final thought on SCP. Frederick Brooks, in his book *The Mythical Man Month*, discusses the second-system effect, which is the tendency of software designers to overcomplicate the second systems that they design:

> As he designs the first work, frill after frill and embellishment after embellishment occur to him. These get stored away to be used "next time." Sooner or later the first system is finished, and the architect, with firm confidence and a demonstrated mastery of that class of systems, is ready to build a second system. This second system is the most dangerous system a man ever designs. When he does his third and later ones, his prior experiences will confirm each other as to the general characteristics of such systems, and their differences will identify those parts of his experience that are particular and generalizable. The general tendency is to over-design the second system, using all the ideas and frills that were cautiously sidetracked on the first one.[1]

It is possible that the designers of SCP were suffering from the second system effect. I2's first major product was Factory Planner, which focused on scheduling within the four walls of a factory. Arguably, SCP represented the second major software effort after FP and looking at the extreme degree of embellishment in that product and its general failure to live up to its stated objectives, it is hard not to conclude that the second system effect was not in some way responsible.

## Endnote

1. Brooks (1995).

# CHAPTER 8

# Calculating Price Elasticity Curves for a Packaged Vacation Tourism Company

The process of building a model is often highly iterative and rapid. You start with something simple, realize that it does not do a good job, and then incrementally add complexity until a reasonable model emerges. The resulting model reflects many adjustments made during the course of model development in response to analyzing model results and validating them against the system being modeled. Often, this process happens over the course of days or weeks, not months, because the client is facing a tight deadline or has a limited budget. The objective is to build a reasonable model in as short a time as possible. Speed is key in this context and we don't have the luxury to cogitate for long periods on the ideal model formulation.

A good case in point is the process I went through constructing price elasticity curves for a tourism company that sells packaged tours to various vacation destinations. We had about four weeks to do all of the work and present a working model to the client. The company wanted to understand the sensitivity of demand for these trips as a function of price. Price elasticity measures the relative change in demand produced by a unit relative change in price. For example, if the price elasticity for coffee is $-0.25$, this means that at the current price of coffee, a 4 percent increase in price will result in only a 1 percent decrease in demand. Generally, price elasticities are negative—an increase in price results in a decrease in demand. This is not always true. For example, for certain luxury items, increases in price can sometimes result in an increase in demand.[1] Typically, though, price elasticities have been shown empirically to range from $-0.2$ to $-3$.

Products with elasticities from about 0 to $-0.8$ are labeled inelastic, those with approximately unit elasticity are in the range $-0.8$ to $-1.2$, and those with elastic demand have elasticities less than $-1.2$.[2]

The company wanted us to calculate price elasticity curves for different trips based on historical sales. They had a large set of historical data which included the price paid for each ticket for each trip relative to a rack rate,[3] the date the ticket was purchased, and the corresponding departure date for the trip. The trips had many attributes associated with them, including departure city, destination city, hotel, and brand. The company sold trips under three different brands, corresponding to different perceived levels of luxury. These brands appealed to different groups of travelers and there was a belief that the brands with higher cachet would tend to have lower price elasticities.

The first thing we did was to aggregate trips into different segments based on specified trip attributes. We initially selected brand, trip destination, and season as the attributes to segment the data. Our hypothesis was that elasticities would logically differ based on these attributes so segmenting the trips in this way provided a way to differentiate elasticities based on different travel segments. At the same time, the segmentation gave us a way to aggregate data across many trips so that we had enough data to analyze each travel segment. Further refinements to segmentation could occur after our initial analysis.

The tickets for each segment were purchased at different discounts from the rack price at different times before departure. A complicated set of business rules dictated the number of tickets offered for sale at a given price a given number of weeks prior to departure. Typically, the company would start offering tickets for sale at least six months prior to departure. The initial pricing would often be moderately discounted over the rack rate. Over the period leading up to about four weeks before departure, the company would typically raise the price as more people would be shopping for vacations during this period. However, as the departure date approached, typically within four weeks of departure, if the number of tickets remaining unsold was high, the company would typically start to discount the tickets, often heavily.

Economics textbooks tell us that price elasticity can be measured by looking at the quantity of a product sold as function of price and fitting this relationship to a curve using regression analysis. In our case, a naïve approach would group all tickets sold for a segment together and construct a price elasticity curve based on the number of tickets bought at each price point. Doing this, we found that elasticities were positive: the smaller the discount from the rack rate, the more tickets that were sold. It is easy to understand why. One of the confounding factors affecting the relationship between tickets sold and price is the time before departure. The pricing policy that the company followed dictated that prices generally rose as the date of departure arrived until close to departure, at which point the ticket prices were discounted. Since most people purchase their tickets one to five months prior to departure, when ticket prices are generally high, the number of tickets purchased at higher prices exceeds the number purchased at lower prices.

So we decided to further segment the data and to look not only at brand, trip destination, and season, but also at number of weeks prior to departure. The result was not what we expected: we still found positive elasticities, meaning more tickets generally sold at smaller discounts from the rack rate even when looking at tickets sold within a given number of weeks prior to departure.

Upon further reflection, we realized that this phenomenon was most likely due to limited availability of tickets in discounted fare classes rather than an inverted relationship between price and demand. In other words, the company limited the number of discount tickets available, so the true demand for tickets at lower prices was not reflected in the number of tickets purchased at these discounted prices.

The next step was to think about how we could adjust the data to accommodate for the fact that the company put a limit on the number of tickets sold at a discount. We came up with the idea of representing demand as a sales rate per day. In other words, rather than counting the number of tickets sold at a given discount, we would calculate a rate of sales per day that tickets were available for sale at the discount. Since the discounted fares were available only on a limited number of days, the rate of sales, normalized by the number of days that they were on sale, would more accurately reflect the demand for discounted sales tickets. By performing a regression analysis on rate of sales as a function of the discount, we were able to obtain a fairly good fit to the data with a negative slope,

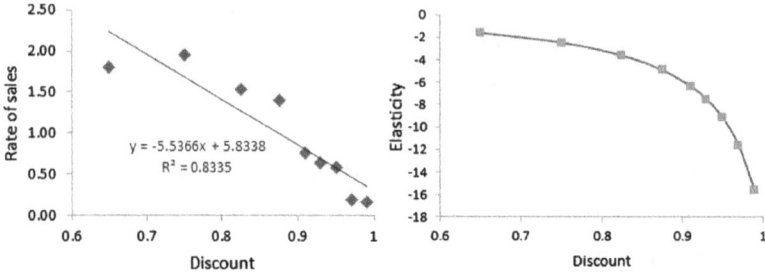

*Figure 8.1  Rate of ticket sales as function of discount for a selected segment along with regression line (left); derived elasticities as function of discount (right)*

as seen in the left of Figure 8.1. The resulting elasticities were, however, quite large, as seen in the right of Figure 8.1.

Were these large (negative) elasticities accurate or were there effects that we had not accounted for in our analysis that amplified the elasticities? As we contemplated the results, we realized there were two problems in our analysis:

1. Our model assumed demand is not constrained. For example, the model says that the rate of sales when prices are not discounted is 0.17 tickets per day but that it would increase by a factor of ~11 if the discount were 0.75. But such an increase is highly unlikely because of capacity constraints and other natural limits on the number of tickets sold during this week.

2. Our model implicitly assumed that the tickets sold in a given time period prior to departure, for example 9 to 10 weeks prior to departure, is independent of other weeks. In reality, introducing a discount in weeks 9 to 10 will, to some extent, pull in sales from future weeks. Or, by the same argument, keeping prices high in weeks 9 to 10 will tend to cause people to wait to see if discounts become available in subsequent weeks. We would actually like to know what the change in demand will be across all time periods if the discount in weeks 9 to 10 is changed, which, because of the cross price elasticity across time periods, will likely be much smaller than the price elasticity within a given period before departure.

We needed a way to adjust the elasticities we calculated to compensate for the overstatement of elasticities due to these two phenomena. One possibility was to normalize these elasticities by calculating an overall elasticity for each travel segment and then adjusting the week-by-week elasticities in such a way that their weighted average corresponded to the overall elasticity. By doing this we are essentially attempting to address the second concern above by saying that the overall effect of a decrease in price in one week will be dampened by the effect of pulling demand forward from subsequent weeks. By making this adjustment, we obtained elasticities that were more modest and more credible.

How did we calculate the overall elasticity for each travel segment? Recall that when we performed a regression of tickets sold as a function of discount for an entire travel segment, we obtained positive elasticities. However, when we performed the same transformation of the data from a ticket quantity to a sales rate as we did when we calculated the elasticities for each week, we obtained more reasonable negative elasticities. So these were the elasticities we utilized to perform our normalization.

The elasticities we calculated were intended to be used by a pricing system that was being developed for the company. We recognized that there was no immediate way to test whether the elasticities we calculated were correct. The intent, however, was to provide some starting values for the system being developed, and that over time, as the company experimented with price changes, they could determine whether the elasticities were accurate.

The development of our model was constrained principally by two factors: the time we had to develop the elasticity model, and the data available to us. In the real world, this is often the case. We don't have the luxury to develop a model which requires data that a company does not collect. Nor do we have the luxury to spend many months developing a model. The solution in this case was certainly not perfect but we made do with the data and time at our disposal and that is often the best that we can do.

It's also important to point out that little in the literature about pricing could serve as a guide for us as we developed our pricing model. The many confounding factors that come into play are not obvious a priori and how to deal with them is not generally dealt with in textbooks. We were left to improvise on our own.

It's also worth mentioning that the process we followed is not one that a data analytics software system could duplicate. I very much doubt that any software system would have been able to come up on its own with the approach we devised. A certain degree of creativity is required to tackle these problems, and analytical software, while it may enable a user already inclined towards creativity to exercise that creativity, does not by itself have any such capabilities.

## Endnotes

1. In general, commonly held beliefs about markets do not hold in the market for luxury goods. I remember having a conversation with an executive at a very high-end retailer who told me they deliberately keep certain items off the display floor and only make them available if a client asks to see them. I asked how the shoppers know to ask and he said that these shoppers tend to be regular customers and the sales staff knows their preferences.
2. Özer and Phillips (2013).
3. The rack rate is the highest price at which tickets for a trip were sold.

# CHAPTER 9

# Understanding the Impact of Variability Through Modeling

Ever since W. Edwards Deming, Joseph Juran, Philip Crosby, and other quality gurus began their crusades over half a century ago, companies have spent considerable energy tracking down and eliminating sources of variability that disrupt their operations and contribute to quality problems. The quality movements—Six Sigma, Total Quality Management, Taguchi Methods, ISO 9000, and others—all hold as a central tenet that a key to quality improvement is the continuous reduction, mitigation, and elimination of factors that contribute to process and system variability. These quality movements are closely aligned with lean manufacturing principles, which focus on the systematic elimination of waste in production. The reduction of system variability is one of the keys to reducing waste or system slack. The reduction in waste in turn translates into reduced costs and production lead time.

The success of these quality programs has led to a generation of managers who rightly view process and system variability as evils to be rooted out. In some ways, these quality programs have been too successful, sidelining as they have almost all discussion about how to cope with the considerable variability that remains in a system even after all controllable sources of variability have been removed. The irony is that while companies have done well at attacking and reducing sources of variability which are under their control, they have generally done a miserable job of managing variability and uncertainty that are either exogenously imposed or are otherwise uncontrollable. Indeed, many managers schooled in the art of quality management might view as an oxymoron the idea of managing variability which cannot be controlled. This is a common mistake. In fact, in the area of managing uncertainty, companies are often their own worst enemies, taking actions or designing systems and business processes that serve only to ignore or amplify the effects of variability.

One example of this phenomenon is the *recency* effect. This is the tendency of people to overemphasize and possibly overreact to recent experiences. By itself, the *recency* effect is just one of many psychological biases that people are subject to. But when people are confronted with random signals, the *recency* effect often causes people to overreact to recent observations. A sales person may adjust his sales projections upward if there has been a recent uptick in sales, even if that uptick is a purely random phenomenon. In the beer game, a popular multi-person game that emulates a distribution network, people often overreact to changes in demand. The fact is that it is often better not to react to variation, especially if the variation is just due to random noise.[1] But this often flies in the face of people's intuition.

By far the single most significant source of uncontrollable variability in a company is demand for its products and services. That is not to say that demand or demand volatility is completely beyond the control of a company. Companies regularly take any number of actions to influence the demand for its products, through pricing actions, advertising, marketing campaigns, and introduction of new or derivative products. But these actions are generally not intended to reduce demand variability and usually have the opposite effect. For example, by providing incentives for customers to buy more products now at the expense of buying fewer products later, a promotional campaign may skew demand over time while not changing overall demand over the periods effected in any significant way. The phenomenon of multiple competitors in an industry taking concurrent actions to increase market share or sales has the unwanted effect of increasing demand volatility overall and for each market participant individually.

Other significant sources of variability include random failures of machinery and equipment, transportation delays, supplier reliability, and rework and scrap due to production or handling failures. The combined effect of different sources of variability on company performance can be surprising and counterintuitive, and it is for this reason that modeling can be of help to understand its implications.

Several years ago, a truck manufacturing company hired us to assess why one of their manufacturing lines was not operating at the level of throughput for which it was designed. The line in question produced truck cabs and was designed to be able to produce 60 cabs per 8-hour shift. The line had been in operation for several years and was never able to come close to reaching this target production rate. The production process consisted of a series of welding and riveting operations performed at stations distributed in a roughly rectangular layout. Parts moved from station to station on jigs connected to an automated conveyor system. Most of the operations at stations were performed by robotic equipment but there were a few operations that were performed by human operators.

The robotic stations were subject to random failure as well as planned maintenance downtime. When one station was down, others could continue to operate to a limited extent, depending on the number of jigs circulating on the automated conveyor system. The more jigs there were, the more cabs that could be moving through the production line at once. On the other hand, with more jigs, the line became ever more sensitive to station failures. The automated conveyor system could only advance a jig if there was an empty space in front of it. With more jigs, the likelihood of being able to advance a jig when a failure occurred grew smaller. The more jigs, the faster the impact of a failure at one station would propagate to other stations, causing them to halt until the repair was completed.

The manufacturing line had been designed and built by an independent manufacturing engineering firm. In designing the line, the company had built a simulation model to determine line throughput based on the specification of the capabilities of the automated conveyor system, the number of jigs circulating on the line, and the operating characteristics of the individual stations on the line, including their estimated failure and repair rates. Their simulation had shown that the line would be able to consistently produce 60 parts per shift. The design firm had presented these results to the company with the usual caveat that its mileage may vary.

It was our job to figure out why the line was not able to achieve its target throughput and make recommendations on specific improvements that would provide the most cost-effective path to reach the target throughput. Our first task was to look at the stand-alone capabilities of each station on the line. For this, we were disappointed to learn that there was little data that existed beyond the design specifications provided by the equipment manufacturers, which we knew from experience would be overly optimistic. The shop floor control system tracked the number of parts processed over time by each station, but this data by itself was not useful for stand-alone analysis because we could not tell how much of the throughput at a station was due to its speed limitation and how much was due to starvation or blockage. We therefore had to spend significant time actually observing each station and taking sample measurements of time to perform each operation.

Failure and repair data presented a different challenge. We could not observe and record failures and repairs at each station. They were, by definition, unpredictable and we could not hope to collect a statistically meaningful sample given our limited time and resources. Fortunately, the maintenance personnel were required to log each failure, to which they responded by recording the time at which they responded to a failure, the reason for the failure, and the time required to make the repair. Unfortunately, this data was recorded the old-fashioned way—pen on paper—and the information had never been transcribed to a computer. We were provided with a stack of papers from each station recording the failures and repairs over the past few months. It was highly imperfect data for all of the reasons one would expect: some entries were illegible, some entries were missing key data like time of failure or time to repair, and all of it was subject to the vagaries of individuals with their own work habits. For example, when recording the failure time, it was up to the individual maintenance person to decide whether to estimate when the failure had occurred at the station or when he or she responded to the failure. Those could be quite different and the form did not try to distinguish between these.

Faced with this stack of papers, I did what any father with young children would do: I put them to work. They happened to be at the perfect age where they could read and write competently but were still innocent enough to not recognize drudgery. And they were perfectly comfortable with computers. The opportunity to help dad with work seemed really exciting. I set up a simple spreadsheet and asked them to translate what was on each handwritten log into the computer. They worked doggedly at this for many hours and saved me considerable effort. Of course, I never told the client about this use of underage labor.

With the data in the computer, I was able to perform some simple statistical analyses to estimate mean time to repair and mean time to fail for each station. I was also able to fit the data to failure and repair distributions.

With the sample data on processing times and failure and repair times, we were able to perform a stand-alone analysis of each station on the line. This analysis confirmed what we suspected: in isolation, each station could produce easily in excess of 60 parts per shift. So, the throughput problem was not simply due to a bottleneck at a specific station or set of stations. Rather, we suspected it was due to the complex interaction effects of station failures on other stations through the constraints of the conveyor system.

At this point, we did not want to simply replicate the simulation model that the design firm had created. After all, their model had shown the line capable of producing 60 parts per shift. On the other hand, it was clear that we needed a model that examined the entire system holistically in order to capture the blocking and starvation effects that we believed were causing the degradation in throughput. We took a closer look at the simulation that the design firm had constructed. A few important details jumped out.

First, the failure and repair times that the design firm had assumed for each station looked far shorter than what we had observed from the maintenance logs. Overall, the total downtime of each station they had assumed looked roughly comparable to the maintenance logs. But they had assumed that the time between failures and the time to repair was much shorter than what we had observed. For example, for one workstation, they assumed failures occurred on average once every two minutes and lasted on average 15 seconds. They also assumed that the failures followed a uniform distribution over a narrow range and the repairs took exactly 15 seconds. This corresponds to a downtime of 11 percent on average. But this was very different from what the maintenance logs revealed. On average, the failures occurred once every four hours and repairs took about 30 minutes. Our statistical analysis of the data showed that failures followed something closer to an exponential distribution and that repairs took time that followed something close to a uniform distribution with a fairly large range. This corresponds to the same downtime—11 percent. But we knew that the scale differences and the differences in distribution would result in very dissimilar line performance.

Second, the design firm's simulation assumed that the number of jigs on the line was fixed at a certain number. In practice, we saw that the number of jigs was quite a bit higher than this number. And we suspected that the number of jigs played a significant role in how random failures propagated throughout the line.

As a result, we undertook to construct a new simulation that would better reflect the actual operation of the line. The results were striking: the simulation showed that the line was incapable of producing anywhere near the 60 parts per shift that the design firm had claimed. The combined effects of significantly underestimating the mean times to failure and repair, mischaracterizing the failure and repair time distributions, and underestimating the number of jigs on the line had led to an overly optimistic assessment of the line's capabilities. The line was in fact operating at the level at which our model predicted. When we validated our model against the actual performance of the line, the results were remarkable: the simulation's prediction of system throughput looked uncannily like the actual factory throughput. Figure 9.1 shows a comparison of actual line throughput versus simulation output. Throughput variability appears to be well captured by the simulation.

With the model in hand, we had the perfect platform on which to test various proposed improvements on line throughput. Through a series of experiments in which we looked at changes to the line without making any assumption about reducing the frequency and duration of station failures, we were able to identify a relatively cost-effective path to improving the line's throughput to 60 parts per shift.

The simulation was also able to demonstrate to management an important concept that had been missing in their discussions about throughput: in a system with variability, throughput is not entirely predictable, as Figure 9.1 demonstrates. The target of 60 parts per shift is not meaningful without some statement of probability or frequency. Is the objective to achieve at least 60 parts per shift on every shift, an average of 60 parts per shift per week, or 90 percent of shifts with between 58 and 62 parts per

**Factory throughput**
Cabs/shift

**Actual**

| Summary Statistics | |
|---|---|
| Mean | 49.05 |
| Median | 50 |
| Mode | 47 |
| Std. Dev. | 4.91 |
| Range | 33 |
| Minimum | 28 |
| Maximum | 61 |

**Simulation**

| Summary Statistics | |
|---|---|
| Mean | 48.93 |
| Median | 49 |
| Mode | 50 |
| Std. Dev. | 4.52 |
| Range | 25 |
| Minimum | 35 |
| Maximum | 60 |

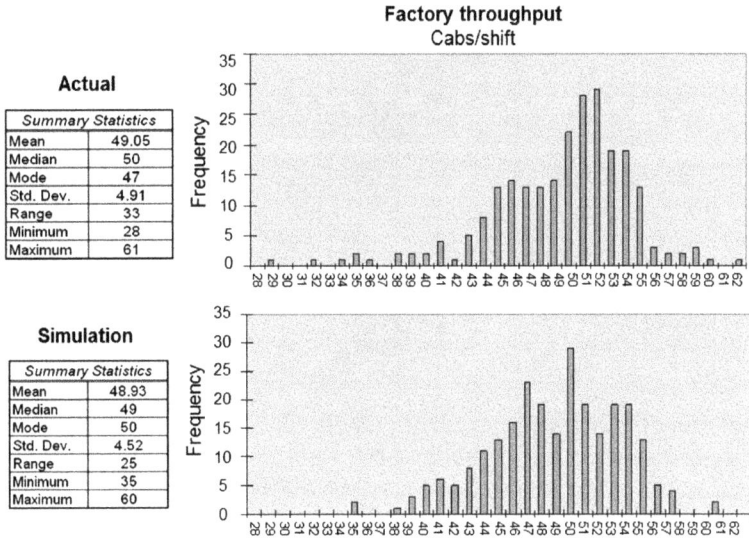

*Figure 9.1  Results of Validation of Factory Simulation*

shift? Each of these are distinctly different objectives. Using simulation output, we were able to construct bar charts of throughput per shift, illustrating to management the range of output that would be expected under normal operation. As a result, we urged management not to fall prey to the *recency* effect; if throughput happened to fall below 60 units for a given shift, which would occur, according to our calculations, on average twice per week, they should not take any immediate action. Rather, they should accept this as part of normal variation in throughput.

## Endnote

1. The funnel experiment that Deming devised illustrates this phenomenon.

# CHAPTER 10

# The Limits of Computer Modeling

To conclude this book, I want to spend some time discussing the theoretical limits of computer models as a way of understanding where computer modeling might go in the future if advances in computer hardware and software engineering continue on their current trajectory.

Today's computers allow unprecedented ability to model complex systems, from natural phenomena such as weather, climate, and protein folding to man-made systems such as airports, hospitals, and manufacturing facilities. The rapid advances in computer hardware and software have fostered an article of faith among many people that computer models can be built to answer any question we might want to answer at any level of detail we desire, if only we apply adequate computational power to the problem. This idea has a strong historical tradition going back at least as far as Laplace, who wrote a brief description of a theoretical automaton that would have unlimited capacity to view the past and future, later dubbed Laplace's demon:

> We may regard the present state of the universe as the effect of its past and the cause of its future. An intellect which at a certain moment would know all forces that set nature in motion, and all positions of all items of which nature is composed, if this intellect were also vast enough to submit these data to analysis, it would embrace in a single formula the movements of the greatest bodies of the universe and those of the tiniest atom; for such an intellect nothing would be uncertain and the future just like the past would be present before its eyes.

Various theoretical arguments have been put forth to refute the idea of Laplace's demon, the acceptance of which would imperil the concept of free will. The implication of Laplace's statement in today's world is that computer models can be built that are accurate to an arbitrary degree of precision, at least in principle. To the extent that this statement has any real meaning, it must be that with ever greater modeling fidelity, we can reduce the uncertainty of the future evolution of the system to an arbitrarily small degree. Weather forecasts will get arbitrarily more accurate as computer models of weather systems improve. Our ability to predict the effectiveness of medical treatments will arbitrarily improve as our models of the human body improve. The ability to detect fraud in credit card transactions will arbitrarily improve until no fraudulent activity will go undetected.

I do not believe this is true, even for a simple system. Take, for example, the problem of estimating failure of a device, like the light bulb in my desk lamp. The Laplace argument would say that if I build models of the light bulb at ever greater degrees of fidelity, these models will get more and more accurate at predicting when the bulb will fail. The limiting case will be a model that will be able to foretell exactly when the bulb will fail. While I do believe that models can be built with ever increasing accuracy, I also believe the asymptotic accuracy of such models does not approach determinism; no model can ever be constructed that will tell me exactly when the light bulb in my desk lamp will fail. In other words, there is inherent uncertainty in the world. How this uncertainty arises is not clearly understood. It may be that the source of uncertainty arises at the subatomic quantum level but if so, the mechanism by which this uncertainty trickles up to the macro world of atoms, objects, and people is not known.

Even in the case of a purely deterministic system, where no uncertainty exists, there is still the phenomenon described by chaos theory that affects computer models: Small deviations in initial conditions can result in huge swings in system evolution. Models with arbitrary precision will still have inaccuracies because arbitrary precision does not mean infinite precision. Any model short of infinite precision has the potential to suffer from the effects predicted by chaos theory. And the idea of constructing an infinite precision computer any time in the future, I think goes well beyond even the most ambitious science fiction fantasy.

## 10.1    The Law of Diminishing Returns

Regardless of what the theoretical limits of computer models are, there is a more practical concern related to model complexity: the law of diminishing returns. As models become more complex, the marginal predictive value of those models decreases. As a practical matter, I believe the marginal predictive value of models decreases quite quickly once a reasonable level of modeling detail is attained. Beyond that point, adding more detail to the model buys you very little increased accuracy at ever-increasing time and cost. When the point of diminishing returns is reached for any given system is difficult to say. It is part of the reason why modeling is more of an art than a science.

The key to effective modeling is to find the sweet spot—the point at which you have gained significant insight from the model, but adding additional detail or complexity does not buy you much and will cost you significantly more. The corollary is that one should always be skeptical of adding complexity to a model for the sake of fidelity. The added fidelity may come at too steep a price and may provide little additional predictive value.

This is an important point to keep in mind in the age of big data. The promise of big data is that we can get more insight by leveraging the increasing quantity of data that companies have at their disposal. If we want to build an ever more accurate regression model to predict, for example, real estate prices in a market, all we have to do is throw additional variables into the regression model and feed the model more data. But as anyone knows who has built regression models, there is a definite point of diminishing returns where adding additional data or variables results in little if any additional model accuracy.

A plausible hypothesis about model complexity versus accuracy is that it follows a curve that is marginally increasing at first, then becomes marginally decreasing. So, if we were to plot model complexity versus accuracy, where the x-axis represents a measure of model complexity and the y-axis measures model accuracy, the curve would look something like what is pictured in Figure 10.1. When the model is first developed, you can get rapid improvements in model accuracy by adding detail. But at a certain point, the addition of complexity starts to have a diminishing impact on model accuracy. Of course, without specific metrics of complexity and accuracy, the exact form of this curve cannot be specified.

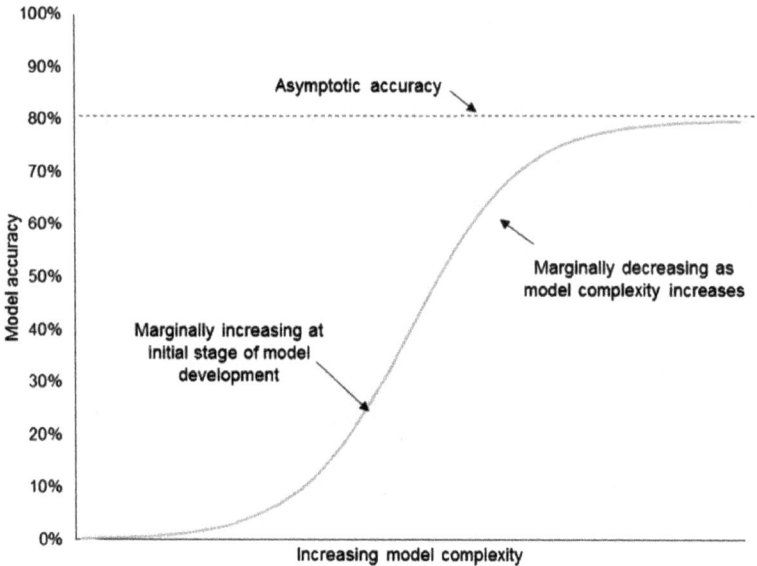

*Figure 10.1* Hypothetical illustration of model accuracy as function
of model complexity

The law of diminishing returns is one of those ideas that seems almost obvious to anyone who has engaged in modeling work. But good empirical evidence for it is surprisingly hard to come by. The climate models in use today for predicting the effects of global warming are a good case in point. These models are perhaps the most complex models ever constructed. General circulation models (GCM), which are the most widely used climate models, are discrete time simulation models that divide the earth into a three-dimensional grid. They apply discretized fluid motion equations to propagate the system forward in time. One critical decision point in the construction of these models is the size of each grid element. All else being equal, the finer the grid, the more accurate the model. But finer grids mean more variables, more computational effort, and more detailed data that need to be fed to the model to specify initial conditions for each grid element. Over time, the spatial and (to a lesser extent) temporal resolution of climate models has increased and this has generally brought greater accuracy, measured in terms of the models' ability to predict past climate patterns. An interesting question is whether the law of diminishing returns applies to GCMs.

Over the past 25 years, the IPCC has released five assessment reports (ARs) on global climate change, in 1990, 1996, 2001, 2007, and 2014. Each of these reports was largely informed by climate models that were available at the time the reports were written. With each successive AR, model complexity has increased as has model accuracy. While I know of no analysis specifically examining whether improvements in accuracy are marginally decreasing, there is research that examines the accuracy of GCMs as function of resolution. This research strongly suggests that the increase in model accuracy appears to be modest compared to the increase in model complexity.

While model complexity is driven by many factors, a reasonable proxy for it is spatial resolution of the atmosphere and oceans. In the *Journal of Climate*, the authors David Masson and Reto Knutti wrote:

> In general, it is not easy to separate the effects of higher resolution and a more comprehensive representation of processes. The groups running models at highest resolution are often also those with the longest experience in building models and with the largest number of people developing the model (of course resolution can be changed, but each model has one or a few standard resolutions that are commonly used and for which it has been optimized). So resolution, rather than just a numerical property, should probably be seen more as an indicator of overall sophistication, effort, computing power, and financial resources going in a model.[1]

In AR1, many climate models used a horizontal grid with cells of about 500 km on a side. In AR2, resolution had improved by a factor of two, with grid cells ~250 km on a side. For AR3, grid cells had been reduced to about 180 km. For AR4, models typically used a 110 km wide grid cell. And for AR5, grid size was approximately 50 km. These are averages, however, and within each AR, significant variation in spatial resolution exists across models.

Vertical resolution has also increased. Typical AR1 models had a single ocean layer and 10 atmospheric layers. AR4 models typically include 30 layers in the oceans and 30 in the atmosphere. The HiGEM AR5 atmospheric model has 38 vertical levels while the ocean model has 40 vertical levels.[2]

As a rough estimate of computational effort, for every twofold increase in horizontal spatial resolution, there is a tenfold increase in computations.[3] If we also account for increased vertical resolution and for added complexity in the way processes are described and for additional processes considered, the increase in computational effort would be significantly greater than the 10x increase from just the increase in horizontal spatial resolution. Looking only at horizontal spatial resolution, the complexity of GCMs, as measured by computations performed, has increased by about 6000 times from AR1 to AR5.

Model accuracy is affected by many factors, not the least of which are the assumptions made about forcing functions from greenhouse gas, aerosol, solar, and volcanic effects. AR2 and earlier models are not as accurate as later models not only because their resolutions were, in general, lower, but because they ignored some forcing functions. Because of these confounding factors, direct comparisons of model accuracy across model generations is problematic.

In the paper by Masson and Knutti, the authors studied the impact of spatial resolution on model accuracy for CMIP3 models (which correspond to AR4 models). These models made roughly the same forcing function assumptions and yet their spatial resolutions varied considerably. Figure 10.2 (left) shows the temperature error of each of the 24 CMIP3 models as a function of their resolution. The straight line is a linear fit to

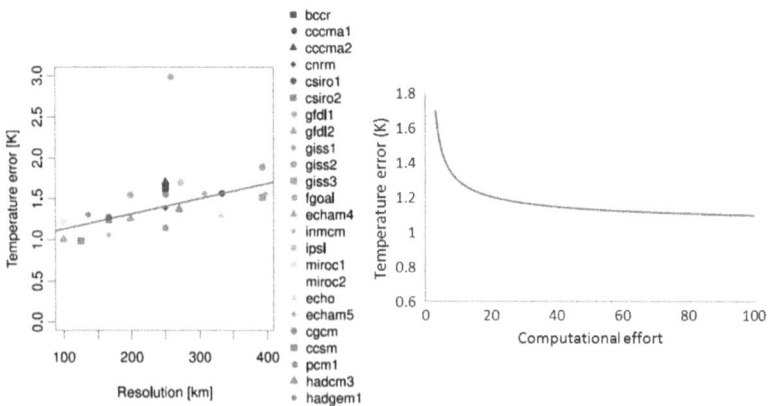

*Figure 10.2 (Left) Temperature error as function of model resolution for 24 CMIP3 models. The straight line is the linear regression line. (Right) Transformation of regression line to reflect computational effort on x axis*[4]

the data. What is evident here is that while higher resolution models tend to be more accurate, the overall improvement in accuracy from 400 km to 100 km is only ~30 percent, while the computational requirements for the 100 km models are at least 100 times greater than the 400 km models, and probably appreciably more than this, after accounting for vertical resolution and added process complexity.

If we view this chart as a log-linear plot, where the x-axis is inversely proportional to the logarithm of computational effort, then by transforming this chart into a linear-linear plot where the x-axis measures increasing computational effort from left to right as in the chart to the right, we see a convex decreasing function, exactly what we would expect if the law of diminishing returns is correct.

It is also worth pointing out that if we were to extrapolate the regression line in Figure 10.2 (left) to 0 km (perfect resolution), we would still be left with an error of about 0.5°C. This provides some empirical evidence for my earlier claim that the asymptotic accuracy of models does not approach perfection as model resolution increases.

This discussion says nothing about whether it is worth the effort to increase the resolution of global climate models. There is no question that the higher resolution models provide much more detailed information about global climate and this additional information may well be worth the additional cost and time spent in developing and running these models. It is simply meant to suggest that in every computer modeling endeavor, the curse of diminishing returns seems to apply.

## 10.2   Optimization Problems will Remain Difficult

Computer hardware and software have advanced rapidly over the last 50 years. And yet many types of large scale optimization problems remain difficult or impossible to solve. For example, the class of NP-hard problems, which include a large number of combinatorial optimization problems, such as the travelling salesman problem, and which arise frequently in business contexts, require enormous computational effort to solve even for moderate sized problems. Clearly, there are NP-hard problems that can be posed that no standard computer, even theoretically, could ever solve. For example, enumerating the entire tree of possible chess games in order to find an optimal strategy using standard computers is impossible, because such a tree would have a number of nodes that exceeds the number of atoms in the universe. If one day a quantum computer can be constructed, then even the most difficult NP-hard problems could in principle be solved relatively quickly. But that day is probably far off in the future.

What does this imply for the solution of optimization problems that arise in business contexts? One consequence is that for the foreseeable future, there will continue to be a need for finding good heuristics to solve these kinds of problems. Heuristics, which are approximate algorithms for finding good, but possibly not optimal, solutions to optimization problems, typically work best when devised for specific problems by exploiting the special structure of these problems. They tend not to work robustly when devised for large classes of problems.

The development of heuristics has until now been an activity that humans have performed. To be sure, the heuristics themselves are implemented in software and performed by computer but an open question is whether computers can be trained to develop heuristics for solving these kinds of optimization problems autonomously. Machine learning techniques, particularly neural networks, have proven to be highly successful in many domains, but it is unclear whether these methods can be applied to the construction of useful heuristics.

## 10.3    Models will not Replace Humans

Science fiction is filled with stories about computers taking control over humans, usually with malevolent intent. Even nonfiction books about the future of computing treat this idea seriously.[5] For this eventuality to occur, it must be the case that computers somehow begin to have volition. It is not enough that they show volition, meaning that they look as if they have volition; we can cleverly program computers to appear as if they have volition but that is very different from having volition. A robot could be programmed to kill people but we would not convict the robot of killing people but rather the programmer who unleashed the robot. When I receive a phone call today from a computer, I don't think, "Oh, a computer has decided to call me today." Rather, I think, correctly, that someone has (annoyingly) programmed this computer to call me.

For computers to have volition, something fundamentally must change in the way computers work. We cannot just say that as computers become more complex, at some point volition and the psychological apparatus underpinning it somehow magically appear inside the computer. To date, computers have shown not one iota of volition and the idea that somehow volition will be emergent as computers get faster strikes me as far-fetched. John Searle made this point when comparing computer emulation to real biological processes:

> Even with a perfect computer emulation of the stomach, you cannot then stuff a pizza into the computer and expect the computer to digest it. Cell-by-cell computer emulation of the stomach is to real digestive processes as cell-by-cell emulation of the brain is to real cognitive processes. But do not mistake the simulation (or emulation) for the real thing.[6]

The point is that computer models, even as they become more and more complex, and more and more realistic, are still just models, not the thing itself. Computers models are useful tools but they themselves will not make decisions unless we instruct them to make decisions. Computers will remain our reliable servant, which does not mean that they will be put to good and proper use, just that they will be put to use. For the foreseeable future, unless computers fundamentally change, we can be sure that behind any malevolence that computers might display, or any havoc that they might wreak, lurk evil human hands.

## Endnotes

1. Masson and Knutti (2011).
2. Schaffrey (2009).
3. http://scied.ucar.edu/longcontent/climate-modeling
4. Masson and Knutti (2011); figure reprinted by permission of Journal of Climate.
5. See, for example, Bostrom (2014) and Floridi (2014).
6. Searle (2014).

# References

Banks, J., Carson, J.S., and Nelson, B.L. (1996). *Discrete-Event System Simulation*. New Jersey: Prentice-Hall Inc.

Bostrom, N. (2014). *Superintelligence: Paths, Dangers, Strategies*. Oxford, United Kingdom: Oxford University Press.

Bratley, P., Fox, B.L., Schrage, L.E. (1987). *A Guide to Simulation*. New York: Springer-Verlag Inc.

Brooks, F. P. Jr. (1995). *The Mythical Man-Month*. Addison-Wesley.

Connors, D.P., Feigin, G.E., and Yao, D.D. (1994). "Scheduling Semiconductor Lines Using a Fluid Network Model." *IEEE Transactions on Robotics and Automation* 10: 88–98.

Connors, D.P., Feigin, G.E., and Yao, D.D. (1996). "A Queueing Network Model for Semiconductor Manufacturing." *IEEE Transactions on Semiconductor Manufacturing* 9: 412–427.

Federgruen, A. and Groenevelt, H. (1988). "Characterization and Optimization of Achievable Performance in Queueing Systems." *Operations Research* 36: 733–741.

Floridi, L. (2014). *The 4th Revolution: How the Infosphere is Reshaping Human Reality*. Oxford, United Kingdom: Oxford University Press.

Forrester, J. (1989). "The Beginning of System Dynamics." *Transcript of Banquet Talk at the International Meeting of the System Dynamics Society Stuttgart, Germany* July 13, 1989. Retrieved from: http://web.mit.edu/sysdyn/sd-intro/D-4165-1.pdf.

Kaner, C., and Bach, J. (2002). *Lessons Learned in Software Testing: A Context Driven Approach*. New York: John Wiley & Sons, Inc.

Knight, F. H. (1921). *Risk, Uncertainty and Profit*. Boston: Houghton Mifflin Co.

Knuth, D. E. (1974). "Computer Programming as an Art." 1974 ACM Turing Award Lecture, Communications of the ACM, 17:12, 667–673.

Knuth, D. E. (1968). *The Art of Computer Programming Vol 1: Fundamental Algorithms*, Third Edition. Reading, Massachusetts (1997): Addison-Wesley.

Law, A.M., and Kelton, W.D. (1991). *Simulation Modeling & Analysis*. New York: McGraw-Hill Inc.

Masson, D., and Knutti, R. (2011). "Spatial-Scale Dependence of Climate Model Performance in the CMIP3 Ensemble." *Journal of Climate* 24: 2680–2692.

Özer, Ö., and Phillips, R. (2013). *The Oxford Handbook of Pricing Management*. Oxford, United Kingdom: Oxford University Press.

Searle, J. R. (October, 2014). "What Your Computer Can't Know." *The New York Review of Books*, 52–55.

Shaffrey, L.C et al. (April, 2009). "U.K. HiGEM: The New U.K. High-Resolution Global Environment Model—Model Description and Basic Evaluation." *Journal of Climate* 22: 1861–1896.

Shanthikumar, G, and Yao, D. (1992). "Multiclass Queueing Systems: Polymatroidal Structure and Optimal Scheduling Control." *Operations Research* 40: 293–299.

Singh, J. (1968). *Great Ideas of Operations Research*. New York: Dover Publications, Inc.

Surowiecki, J (March, 2003). "The Wages of War." *The New Yorker*, 33.

Whittaker, J., Arbon, J., and Carollo, J. (2012). *How Google Tests Software*. New Jersey: Pearson Education, Inc.

# Index